HIDDEN HEROES 2

THE GOOD NEWS
MUST GO OUT

True Stories of God at Work in
the Central African Republic

THE GOOD NEWS MUST GO OUT

True Stories of God at Work in the Central African Republic

REBECCA DAVIS

CF4•K

10 9 8 7 6 5 4 3
Copyright © 2011 Rebecca Davis
Paperback ISBN: 978-1-84550-628-5
Epub ISBN 978-1-78191-847-0
Mobi ISBN 978-1-78191-1-848-7

Published in 2011, reprinted in 2016 and 2017
by Christian Focus Publications,
Geanies House, Fearn, Tain,
Ross-shire, IV20 1TW,
Great Britain

Cover design by Daniel van Straaten
Cover illustration by Fred Apps
Other illustrations by Fred Apps
Printed and bound by Nørhaven, Denmark

*Cover picture is Mananga the Wood and Water Boy on his way to share the
message of Jesus with the people at Saras' village. This story can be found in
Chapter 10.*

*To the tireless workers of Baptist Mid-Missions
who follow in the footsteps of the pioneers,
and to my brothers and sisters
of the Central African Republic.
I look forward to meeting you someday.*

HIDDEN HEROES SERIES

Hidden Heroes 1: *With Two Hands:*
True Stories of God at Work in Ethiopia
ISBN: 978-1-84550-539-4

Hidden Heroes 2: *The Good News Must Go Out:*
True Stories of God at Work in the Central African Republic
ISBN: 978-1-84550-628-5

Hidden Heroes 3: *Witness Men:*
True Stories of God at Work in Papua, Indonesia
ISBN: 978-1-78191-515-8

Hidden Heroes 4: *Return of the White Book:*
True Stories of God at Work in Southeast Asia
ISBN: 978-1-78191-292-8

Hidden Heroes 5: *Lights in a Dark Place*
True Stories of God at Work in Colombia
ISBN: 978-1-78191-409-0

Hidden Heroes 6: *Living Water in the Desert*
True Stories of God at Work in Iran
ISBN: 978-1-78191-563-9

To access more information and activities about
The Good News Must Go Out, see the Christian Focus
website at www.christianfocus.com

Contents

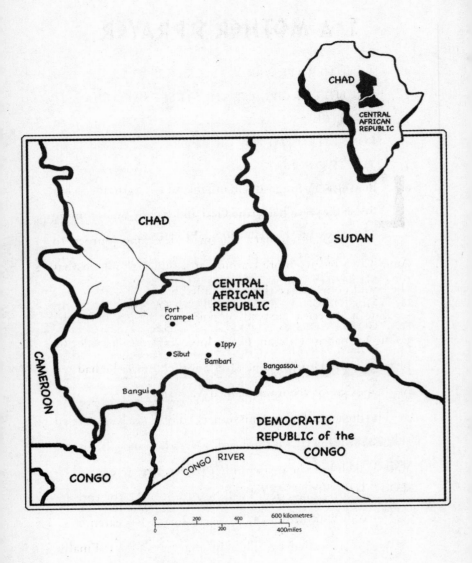

1. A MOTHER'S PRAYER

Long ago, a young woman in Finland felt a stirring in her heart to serve her great God and Savior by becoming a foreign missionary. She made the long journey to America to receive more training at a Bible school, so that she could go wherever the Lord called her.

But in America, instead of going to Bible school, the young woman met a man, fell in love, and got married. She began to have children, one after another, until she had ten of them. One of them was named Margaret.

The dream of being a missionary? This lady had married a man who didn't love the Lord. Over the years the dream almost died, but she just couldn't forget it.

"Oh, Lord," she cried, "will You forgive me for turning aside? Will You restore the years the locust has eaten?"

The years rolled by. The children grew older. Finally, the lady's husband came to the Lord just days before he died.

"Oh, Lord!" she cried. "Will You call one of my children to take Your good news to another country where Your Name has never been heard? Will You show me that You have forgiven me?"

One by one the children entered their teen years and began to talk of college and marriage and business.

And the woman, now not so young, continued to pray.

See Thinking Further for Chapter 1 on page 146.

2. THE BUTTON GIRL AND THE STREET SWEEPER

So what in the world am I doing here? Margaret didn't dare utter the words, but she sighed deeply as she slid into the pew beside her friend. It had been a year and a half since she had seen the inside of this church building, and she wouldn't have come now except that her friend had begged her.

Margaret felt a flush of guilt as she thought about Miss Jessie Robbins, the sweet lady who had told her about Jesus. Miss Robbins had shown Margaret her own sin and her need for a Savior. She had shown Margaret that Jesus was the only way.

But then, after Margaret had become a Christian, Miss Robbins had wanted her to become a missionary.

A missionary! Margaret had recoiled at the thought. Why, she knew what happened to missionaries. They got boiled in a pot and *eaten*. Oh, no, that absolutely was not for her. As much as she liked Miss Robbins, Margaret had started avoiding her. In fact, she had even quit going to church.

A year and a half had passed, and Margaret had tried not to think about God.

But now, here she was. Waiting for the meeting to start. She heaved another sigh and swung her leg vigorously. In a way it felt good to be back, she had to admit. And maybe the speaker would be interesting. A converted Jew.

Now the pastor was introducing him. "Mr. Flacks has been from the bottom to the top to the bottom again," he said. "From a penniless Polish immigrant to one of the richest men in the Midwest, to a penniless Bible student. But he *found Christ*."

Yes, she could tell it was going to be interesting. Mr. Joseph Flacks described his life in New York City, his rise in wealth, his move to St. Louis, and his marriage to a beautiful woman. It all captured Margaret's attention. But then he began to tell a story that captured more than her attention.

"This little girl who worked for me in my clothing factory," he said, "she was thirteen years old. Thirteen, mind you. And all she did was sew on buttons. She was the lowest of my employees. But she was brave enough to invite me to go hear that famous evangelist, Gypsy Smith.

"Can you guess how I responded? Me, the important, rich businessman, go listen to that crazy preacher? I laughed at her. Yes, I did. I laughed right in her face.

"But ladies and gentlemen, let me tell you something. That little girl, as young and small and scared as she was, she did not give up. She asked me again the next day. And the next. And the next. For *nine days in a row*, she invited me to come to those meetings, even though I said no every single time. That's right.

"Then, on the next-to-the-last day of the meetings when I refused her again, she burst into tears. Yes, she did. Through her tears, she told me that if I didn't receive Jesus, I would go to hell.

"My heart was so touched by her concern that I canceled my dinner engagement and went with her to the meeting. I went the next night too. Yes, I did. And by the end of it all, ladies and gentlemen, I was a changed man. I saw that my riches and my social standing meant nothing before God. I needed Jesus."

Mr. Flacks went on. He talked about how coming to Christ brought disaster in his life. He lost his riches, he lost his social standing, he even lost his wife.

But Margaret could barely hear the rest of the story. Her heart was captured by that thirteen-year-old button girl.

"Oh God!" she prayed. "I'm so ashamed! What love she showed! She could be brave in the face of that big important man's mocking, and here I am, nineteen years old and doing nothing for You. Nothing! I'm so ashamed! I know nothing about the kind of love she poured out!"

By the time Margaret turned her attention back to the speaker, he was telling the story of going to Moody Bible Institute with no money. This once-distinguished businessman began to sweep streets in order to pay his school bill. "As you know, it's a very important job," he added wryly.

The crowd murmured with subdued laughter. Now, in 1917, cars were quickly replacing horses, but in those earlier days, street sweeping was an extremely important job. The street sweeper had to be up by two o'clock in the morning to sweep away all the horse manure from the streets before the new day's traffic began. This was one of the lowest jobs in all of society.

"Christ poured out His love on me," Mr. Flacks continued. "Could I not at least give my dignity for Him?"

Margaret's heart burned, and she hid her face in her hands. "Oh God!" she silently cried. "I'm so ashamed! Forgive me, Lord Jesus! Restore the time I have wasted!"

I need to meet this man. Margaret waited until almost everyone had left. Her heart in her throat, she walked up to him. What would she say? But when she finally reached out to shake his hand, the words that came out of her mouth were not the words she expected. "I want to go to Moody Bible Institute!"

Mr. Flacks seized her hand and held it. "Do you really mean it?"

"Uh . . . yes, I think so," Margaret answered, surprised at herself. "I never even heard of Moody Bible Institute until tonight."

"I'll be in town two more weeks. Come to my Bible studies at noon, and we'll talk."

So Margaret went. She studied with Mr. Flacks, and she talked with him. "But I can't really do this, you know," she said one day. "My mother is a widow and I help to support the family, and there are ten of us children, so I just don't know how. . . ."

"I'll help you," Mr. Flacks answered. "If the Lord wants you to do this, you must not be afraid. I'll go with you to tell your mother."

Margaret's heart felt heavy. Poor Mother! What would Mother do, discovering she was losing a daughter to go to Bible school and then maybe to be a missionary?

So Mr. Flacks went with Margaret to her house. "Mrs. Nicholl," he said, "what would you say if I told you that

Margaret wants to pour out her life as an offering to the Lord?"

Margaret's stomach tied in a knot, waiting for her mother's answer.

"I would say, 'Praise the Lord!' " Mrs. Nicholl's eyes welled with tears. "It would be an answer to my prayer, a prayer I've prayed for many long years." She pulled out her cotton handkerchief and dabbed at her eyes. "Mr. Flacks," she said, "if Margaret chose to be a missionary, it would be one of the happiest days of my life."

See Thinking Further for Chapter 2 on page 146.

3. THIRD CLASS

Margaret settled in her seat with her face to the window as the creaky train laboriously chugged away. She gazed out at the strange birds sitting on odd trees squawking unfamiliar noises.

As the landscape of Africa drifted by, Margaret thought over the last five years, years that had swept past her like this landscape. Two amazing years at Moody Bible Institute. Then on to nursing school. Then she had to choose whether to go with a mission group that would support her fully, or if she should go with this new faith-only mission, with the long name of "The General Council of Cooperating Baptist Missions of North America".[1]

With Hudson Taylor as her example, Margaret had chosen to live by faith. After she made this decision, a family from her small church had committed to support her. Yes, God was providing.

---

[1] Their name was later changed to Baptist Mid-Missions.

After that she spent time in France, preparing to work in French Equatorial Africa, where the French government was in charge.

Then the long boat ride, almost a month, with four other new missionaries and Mr. Haas, the founder of the mission group. Now in 1923, Mr. Haas had been working in Africa for several years already. His skin looked sallow and his brilliant blue eyes sunk deep into his face from all the fevers he had suffered, but when he smiled, his face lit up the room.

It was on the boat that Margaret first told Mr. Haas the story of Mr. Flacks and her call into ministry. "You can't imagine how surprised I was," she said, "when I found out my mother actually wanted me to go! She had been praying for one of her children to go!"

"Ha Ha!" Mr. Haas threw back his head, and his bushy red beard shook with laughter. "We knew you were chosen of God to come with us! That's the very same thing my mother said to me! I was afraid to tell her that God wanted me to go to Africa, and she said, 'Oh, but son, I've been praying that God would call you to Africa!' So yes, my sister, I can imagine how surprised you were, because I was surprised the same as you!"

And now they were on the train, chugging slowly along, gazing at the parrots and monkeys. Almost to the Congo

River, where a boat would take them to the French colony of Ubangi-Shari.[2] Their final destination.

As she gazed out the window, Margaret felt a tap on her shoulder and jumped a little. Her thoughts were jolted back to the present, and she turned to see one of the other missionaries. "Margaret, you haven't seen Mr. Haas, have you?"

"No, isn't he in this train car here with us?"

"I thought he was, but look around, and you'll see that he isn't."

Margaret got out of her seat to see one of the men of their group coming from the end of the train car. "He's not riding second class," the man said. "He's riding *third* class."

---

[2] When this colony gained its independence in 1960, it became known as the Central African Republic.

"Third class?" Margaret said, working her way down to the end of the car. "Isn't that the open flat car?"

"Yep! No railings, nothing! Just boards! Go look! He's doing his mission work, even now!" Margaret looked out. Of course Mr. Haas already knew the African language of Sango, so there he was, with the many Africans who were riding third class, teaching them a song in their native language. She recognized the tune.

There is a fountain filled with blood, drawn from Immanuel's veins,
And sinners plunged beneath its flood lose all their guilty stains.

The Africans must have learned the song quickly, because they were already singing it, in a mystical chant-like wail that she could hear even over the chugging of the train. They closed their eyes and swayed from side to side, even with no railings.

And then Margaret watched Mr. Haas talk and talk, waving his arms and pointing into the sky and holding up his big black Bible. She watched the faces of the Africans, listening in rapt attention, some of them even with their mouths hanging open at this amazing story of salvation. *They must be hearing the good news for the very first time.*

When the train needed fuel and had to stop to get more wood, all the third-class passengers were supposed to jump down and chop. Usually only Africans traveled third class, but today Mr. Haas was with them. He jumped down with them and chopped too, singing as he worked, even in this terrible heat. The others joined in, in their haunting African chant. Singing of the blood of Jesus. *I am watching a lesson of love.* Margaret never forgot it.

As she settled back into her seat, Margaret thought about some of the things Mr. Haas had taught them. *I know French is the official language in all this part of Africa,* she thought. *And that's the language I learned. But he's right. Sango is the way to reach the people.*

A long boat ride up the Congo River, full of hippos and crocodiles, took them to the village of Bangui, the capital of Ubangi-Shari.

"It's a hundred miles inland to our mission station in Sibut, Margaret," Mr. Haas said. "Most of the ladies travel by push-push."

Margaret eyed the one-wheeled contraption with a seat in the middle. One African pushed on the handles behind, and another one pulled on the handles in front. "A push-pull, I think rather," she said. "And I'm almost six feet tall. I think I'm too big for those Africans to either push me or pull me. I'm glad I brought my bicycle."

While the other missionaries walked or sat in the precarious push-push, Margaret threw her leg and heavy skirt over the bar of her bicycle. She steadied herself and began cycling down the long narrow path, one hundred miles through the ten-foot-high grass to the mission station.

See Thinking Further for Chapter 3 on page 147.

4. KONGI THE GOAT BOY

Mr. Rosenau, the mission leader, looked at Margaret in surprise. "A woman?" he sputtered. "I thought you were bringing another man. He was going to share a room with Mr. Metzler."

"Well, obviously she can't do that," Mr. Haas answered calmly. "What will we do?"

"I don't know. Maybe the goat house?" Mr. Rosenau pointed up the slope. "It's just been cleaned."

Margaret propped her bicycle against an odd-looking tree, very thick and tall, and wiped the sweat from her forehead. Every inch of her heavy dress felt as if it were sticking to her body. Unlacing her shoes, she pulled them off, and her socks, too. Ah, the moist dirt felt cool under her feet. Maybe the African custom of going barefoot wasn't such a bad idea!

Then she gazed around at the mission station on the hill at Sibut. It had been started two or three years earlier, so

there were already three small, neat mud-block houses and a chapel in the large circular clearing. At the center was a blackened fire circle, and Margaret could picture Africans and missionaries sitting together around it at night, singing.

Mrs. Rosenau, a thin, frail woman, joined Margaret, speaking in low tones. "This very hill," she said, "was the site of the witchdoctor's cannibal feasts."

Margaret shuddered. People really had been eaten. Right here.

"But now," Mrs. Rosenau continued, "they feast on the Word of God. Look at the people."

Margaret watched the Africans around the mission station, carrying wood, caring for animals. Their bright white smiles split their dark faces, and their laughter came easily. "They're very happy," she said.

"Yes, they are. But they used to live in fear. Now these people know Jesus, and it has changed their lives. Not all of them, but many."

"I want so much to talk with them. Do any of them know French?"

"Very few, and very little. They can't pronounce our names, so they call all the missionary ladies 'mama.' I've finally gotten used to it, but I'm sure it will sound strange to you."

"Maybe a little," Margaret chuckled. "But I hope I can be a spiritual mama to some of them before long."

"But most likely you'll have to learn Sango to do it."

"Yes, I know." Margaret glanced back toward the chapel, where the two missionary men were still talking and gesturing. "Looks like I'll be working on it in the goat house." She uttered a low laugh. "Well, Lord, You told me to be ready for anything."

Mr. Haas came bounding toward Margaret, his bright blue eyes alight. "I'm sure you heard all that, didn't you, Margaret? It will be better than it sounds. We'll whitewash it and put sand on the floor, and you'll have yourself a first-rate little hut."

"I'm sure it will be fine," Margaret murmured.

It wasn't long until she was able to carry her satchels past the goats and right into their house. "Shoo! Shoo away now!" she cried. "Go!" She waved her arms at the goats and finally closed the door.

Bang! Bang! There they were, butting their heads against the flimsy bamboo.

"Shoo!" she opened the door and chased them a few steps. The goats ran off a bit and stood and watched her. "Go!" She grabbed an old dress from her satchel and waved it at them, hoping to scare them. Then she closed the door again.

Bang! Bang! They were back, and they wanted in.

Oh, well, she finally thought with a sigh, *I think I can ignore them.* She began to sing as she unpacked her lockers, trying to sing in rhythm with the banging.

But nighttime was different. Margaret didn't want to sing, she just wanted to sleep. But the goats were still there. Bang! Bang! Every few seconds, it seemed.

"Mr. Rosenau, I simply can't sleep because of those goats," Margaret said the next morning. "I don't mean to complain. I really don't want to be a complainer. But I have to be able to sleep or I won't be able to study."

"Oh, my goodness, yes, yes, certainly," Mr. Rosenau answered. "We need to do something about that." He thought for a moment. "I think I can hire a goat boy to stand guard and keep the goats away from your hut."

The next day Kongi appeared, dressed in ragged shorts and a jaunty cap. He looked about ten, and he stood shyly gazing up at Margaret, his hands behind his back, his toes digging into the dirt. In broken French he asked, "Do you need a goat boy, Mama?"

"Oh! You speak French!" Margaret exclaimed. "We shall have some fun now!" She brushed the sweaty strands of brown hair from her eyes and knelt down. "Listen, Kongi," she said. "You know French, right?"

Kongi nodded vigorously. "A little, Mama," he answered.

Laying her hands on his thin shoulders she said, "I want to learn Sango. Oh, it would be so wonderful if I had my own teacher. Will you teach me?"

Kongi's face lit up, and he laughed right out loud. "I will teach the missionary mama?" he exclaimed. "The small boy will teach the big lady!"

"Yes, the 'big lady' is right." Margaret made a wry face. "But no matter. We will learn together."

"You read to me in French," Kongi suggested, "and I will tell you the Sango words. Then you can learn. Do you have a book?"

"Of course I have a book!" Margaret leaped to her feet and almost ran back into the goat shed. "Shoo! Shoo!" she hollered as she ran. Then she came running back out with a French Bible. "This is the book I will read. Kongi, do you know Jesus?"

"No, Mama," Kongi answered. "But I have heard of Him."

"French and Sango will be used of God today." Margaret spoke almost under her breath. "I will take you to Jesus." Together the small teacher and the big student settled under the shade of a tree to read the Word of God.

Every night Kongi slept in front of the goat shed with a stick. Every day Margaret read to Kongi from the gospel of Mark, telling the amazing stories of Jesus. She read, Kongi spoke, she wrote. Sometimes Kongi puzzled over a word, sometimes they had to run to the Rosenaus' house for help. Sometimes they both doubled over laughing at a mistake. But mostly they talked about Jesus. They talked and talked. Kongi asked questions. And Margaret answered.

"Mama," Kongi said one day, "if Jesus really did this for me, if He lived and died and rose again for me, I must believe. I must give Him my life."

"Yes, Kongi." Margaret felt almost breathless. "And He will change your life forever."

Immediately Kongi threw himself onto the ground and spread out his hands. "Oh, Jesus," he cried out, "You are my God! This is my life!"

Then he looked up, his eyes shining. "Thank you, Mama," he said. "I give you Sango, but you give me Jesus."

"Yes, Kongi." Margaret put her hand over her racing heart. She felt as if it would burst with joy. "That's why I came. That's why we all came. Wait a minute." She ran inside and back out again. "This is for you. It is the New Testament of the Bible."

"For me?" Kongi was amazed. "And you will teach me to read it?"

"Yes, I will." Margaret quickly wrote a short inscription in the front.

Kongi leaned his head against Margaret. "I will be your goat boy forever, Mama."

"Oh no!" Margaret put her arm around him and gave him a squeeze. "No, that wouldn't be right. You'll grow up and serve Jesus however He wants you to."

"But for now, I will be your goat boy."

"Yes, for now. And we'll keep learning together."

See Thinking Further for Chapter 4 on page 147.

5. THE TWO SULTANS

Margaret looked around at the small buildings here in Sibut, the place she had learned to call home. "Somehow it seems like four months isn't long enough," she muttered under her breath. "I'm not sure I know the Sango language well enough to start a school to teach French to the natives." She threw her satchel into her bicycle basket. "But Mr. Haas wants us to keep pressing on to the interior. Oh, Lord Jesus, for your glory, I want to keep pressing on too. I certainly didn't come to Africa to be comfortable."

With hugs and tears she said good-bye to the missionaries she had lived with as family for this brief time. She gazed through the trees where she knew lay many villages that she had biked to, day after day, to proclaim the gospel in French and in her broken Sango. "Will the others go to those villages?" she wondered.

Then she watched as the African porters carried her five foot lockers out of her little goat shed, holding all her worldly goods. "Well, it's only three hundred fifty miles," she murmured. "That should be only a couple of weeks on my bike. Oh, God, thank You for physical endurance." She hiked up her skirt and climbed on. "Are you ready, Kongi?"

"Coming, Mama!" the little goat boy ran ahead, carrying the other satchel.

Pressing on, the troop made the trip in only twelve days. Exhausted, Margaret finally landed at the mission station at Bangassou. Every muscle ached, and she fell into the bed the welcoming missionary lady offered her.

But a terrible noise of screaming and beating drums kept her awake all night. Hour after hour the wails and shrieks pierced the night. Margaret would begin to fall asleep from exhaustion and suddenly be jolted awake again, her heart pounding.

"What in the world was it?" she asked Mrs. Becker the next morning.

"I'm so sorry," the missionary answered. "You must dress quickly, though, because we're supposed to meet the French administrator today."

"Yes, yes, I will," said Margaret. "But will I be treated to that serenade every night?"

"For three nights a month, I'm afraid. They dance on the sultan's grave at the full moon. It's their way of honoring him. Dress quickly, and I'll take you to see it on the way to meet the French officials."

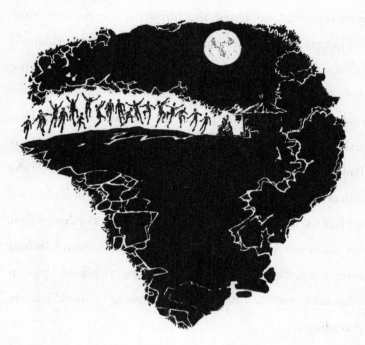

Full of curiosity, Margaret donned her nicest dress and combed and pinned her thick brown hair into a neat bun at her neck. As they walked to the government post, Mrs. Becker pointed to a hill. "There it is." It was a huge cement circle, with the grass around it all trampled down.

"Why is it so large?" Margaret asked. "Why is it all cemented?"

"He was a sultan," came the reply. "When he died, he was so important that three hundred of his wives were buried alive with him, along with much food."

"Three hundred women buried alive!" Margaret could hardly imagine such a thing. "How long ago was this?"

"Oh, almost twenty years ago now. Before any Christians had brought the name of Jesus. And even now, well, these traditions die hard."

"I can't even . . . I can't even. . . ." Margaret was speechless. As they continued on their way, she looked up at the brilliant blue sky to try to chase out the image, but her mind was still filled with the picture of three hundred women wordlessly trooping down a long flight of steps to their dark death. "Oh, God!" she breathed. "How great is that darkness!"

"I have a story to tell you," Mrs. Becker said as they walked. "When I first arrived here two years ago, I was alone, and I was the first white woman these Africans had ever seen. I didn't know that I was building my house on the sultan's grave."

"You built . . . you built your house *there*?"

"Yes, and I couldn't understand why the Africans avoided me. They didn't try to kill me, they just didn't talk to me. But after three months I finally found out.

For three months they had been working to get me off that land with their spells and sacrifices. They started with small ones because, they thought I was only a woman, and they thought that the spirit of the dead sultan would drive me away. But when that didn't work, they kept offering bigger sacrifices and trying stronger spells, but nothing worked. Then finally, after three months, they gave up, and a lot of them came to me to find out what my power was that was so much greater than theirs. The Lord gave me a great harvest."

Margaret let out a deep breath. "That was an open door, wasn't it?"

"Exactly." Mrs. Becker smiled. "That was the promise the Lord had given me through those long difficult months. 'Behold, I have set before thee an open door, and no man can shut it!' "

But then she sighed. "Unfortunately, the French government told me to move. I had to obey them without question. They cemented the grave as a 'memorial' to the sultan. Makes it much more convenient for dancing on in the full moon." Her words had a hard edge. "Oh, this is Administrator Eboue's office. Don't forget to curtsy."

A stocky black man dressed in a dark blue uniform greeted them in French. "So this is the new missionary." He bowed.

"Yes, sir," Margaret bent her knee respectfully. "Margaret Nicholl."

"Welcome, Miss Nicholl." Mr. Eboue sat down. "Did you visit the grave of the sultan on the way here?"

"Uh, yes, sir." Should she let him know how appalled she was? Or should she act as if it were all perfectly normal?

"Really, Miss Nicholl, I see from your face what you think of the people of Bangassou. And certainly, we want them to change too. But these changes come bit by bit."

"They come by the gospel of Jesus Christ!" Margaret answered boldly.

"Yes, as you say." The black Frenchman nodded slowly. "Perhaps you would like to meet that sultan's son. He is coming here for a large dinner party in a few days, after visiting in Europe."

Once again Margaret tried to picture something she could hardly imagine. An African sultan. How would he dress? Would he look like a witchdoctor? What kind of warpaint and animal skins would he wear to a government dinner? How would he act? Would his anger blaze against his father for causing his own mother to be buried alive? Or would he be plotting for his own three hundred wives to follow him to the grave?

A few nights later, with trepidation, Margaret approached the French administrator's house. Was she ready for this dinner? Was she ready to meet Sultan Hetman? "Let me shine forth Jesus, O Lord," she breathed.

"Good evening, Mademoiselle Nicholl." There stood a handsome black man, dressed in a perfect white uniform spangled with medals. He spoke perfect French.

Margaret tried to collect her wits. "Uh . . . uh . . . it is good to meet you, Sultan Hetman."

"I understand you were troubled at the sight of my father's grave."

How should she answer? "Uh, yes, I was." Should she say more? "I felt very sorry for those women." There. She said it.

The young sultan nodded in response. "My father was able to have whatever he wanted. He could take any woman he chose. He could tell anyone to bow to him. He struck fear into the heart of anyone who came close." Sultan Hetman offered his arm and led Margaret to the large table, decorated with crystal goblets, china plates, and many pieces of silverware. "But my father was a miserable, angry man." He pulled out her chair and helped her get seated. Then he sat down on the other side of the table and leaned toward her. "My father was filled with torment."

Sultan Hetman sat up straight and unfolded his embroidered linen napkin gracefully on his lap. "I, on the other hand, have only one wife, to whom I am faithful. I ask no one to bow and scrape to me. I doubt that I strike fear into anyone's heart." He laughed gently. "But, Mademoiselle, I am a happy man. I am at peace. And I want all the people of my land to know the peace I have found."

Sultan Hetman's dark eyes lit up with a brilliant fire. "My peace has come because the heart of one man was filled with a love for God and touched with the need to come to the darkness of Africa with the light of the gospel. Mademoiselle, I learned of Jesus from your Mr. Haas. My life has never been the same."

See Thinking Further for Chapter 5 on page 148.

6. JIGGERFOOT

Margaret hesitated on the path. "What in the world? What little creature is that?" It was bouncing around on the path in the most unusual way, swaying from one side to the other and occasionally hopping. Was it a chimpanzee? No. It was a little boy, maybe six years old.

"Hello!" she called in Sango. "Greetings!"

The boy turned and looked at her. As she drew closer she could see that his dark eyes looked as sad as any she had ever seen. But he just stood there in the narrow path, swaying and hopping.

"What is your name, little boy?" Margaret asked gently.

The boy turned his mournful eyes downward and answered. "Jiggerfoot."

An odd name! Margaret looked down at his feet and gasped. Both of his feet were huge and swollen. Some of his toes were even missing. No, it wasn't leprosy. It was the worst case of jiggers she had ever seen. No telling how many of those horrible little insects had burrowed their way under his skin.

"Oh, you poor little thing!" she cried. "Your mama doesn't take care of you?"

"No mama," he answered.

"What about your daddy?"

"No daddy," he answered.

"Well, where do you live? How do you get food?"

"Live no place," said Jiggerfoot. "Get food by stealing."

Margaret knelt down. How skinny this poor little thing was! "Listen, Jiggerfoot," she said. "I'm a nurse. I love to help little boys. If you go up to my house and wait for me, I can help your feet get better as soon as I get back."

Jiggerfoot rolled his eyes toward the sky. "Mmmm" was all he said.

With frustration Margaret realized that as soon as she walked away, he would probably disappear. *How can I get him to go, Lord?* Oh, yes, the bananas! *Thank you, Lord!*

"Listen, Jiggerfoot. On my porch there's a great big bunch of ripe bananas. You can go up there and eat all you want. If you see my goat boy, tell him that Mama Margaret told you to do it."

For the first time, the little boy's eyes lit up. Without another word he started lolloping up the path that Margaret had just come down.

It wasn't long before the missionary returned from her errand. Would he be there?

She shouldn't have wondered. There he was, eating a banana, with *two dozen* banana peels scattered around him.

"Hello, Jiggerfoot!" she called.

The little boy rolled his eyes toward her but said nothing.

"Will you let me help your feet?"

He didn't move.

"I'll be right back," Margaret promised. She ran inside her hut and came back with a large basin of pinkish water.

"We're going to soak your feet in this stuff. It will clean them so I can get those jiggers out."

Jiggerfoot sat silent, but he let the missionary lady gently put his feet in the water. While she washed them, she talked.

"I don't know if you've ever heard of Jesus, Jiggerfoot, but He's the best news I could ever give you."

Jiggerfoot took a bite of another banana and gazed intently at the lady who was washing his feet.

"He's the Son of the true God. There is a true God, you know. The One who made everything around you."

Jiggerfoot said nothing.

"The true God is far more powerful than the spirits," Margaret went on. "But the best thing about Him is that He is a God of love."

Suddenly the boy spoke. "Love?" He turned his face away and threw the banana peel far from him.

"Yes, like your mama—" Margaret stopped herself, remembering that he had no mother. "I mean, like you see mamas showing to their babies."

For half an hour Margaret washed and talked while Jiggerfoot said almost nothing. She felt her own heart beginning to swell with love for this little thief.

"Now, listen," she said. "Your feet are clean. Now I'm going to get those jiggers out. It's going to hurt. And it will probably take a long time. But when I get done, your feet will be well. The jiggers will be gone."

Margaret disappeared into the hut once more while the little boy waited. When she returned, she was carrying a tray of needles and other equipment. Then she sat down and took Jiggerfoot's foot in her lap.

"It's going to hurt," she said again. Oh, how much it hurt, she knew. She looked at the little foot. Each toe was dark and hot and lumpy with the embedded bugs. Now she had to prick holes all around each flea, swollen huge with eggs, in order to lift it out without breaking it. If it broke open, the toe would be filled with even more infection.

She picked up a needle and gently poked Jiggerfoot's toe, expecting him to cry out. But he gripped the stool he was sitting on and remained quiet.

Margaret concentrated on her work so hard that she was only occasionally able to speak. But when she did, she knew what to say.

"Jesus was the Son of God, and He came to earth to show His love. One of the ways He did it was by healing people." She looked up from her close work. "Jesus could heal people with just a word! I wish I could do that!" For the first time, a glimmer of a smile touched the little boy's face.

For half an hour Margaret worked and talked, knowing that every touch hurt like fury. Finally when she looked up, she saw that a tear was running down Jiggerfoot's face.

How brave he is! she thought. *Other children would have screamed about this!* "That's enough for this morning," she said then. "We can do some more this afternoon. I have some rice for you."

Again she thought she saw the glimmer of a shy smile.

Jiggerfoot ate his rice with Kongi, saying nothing as the goat boy talked to him. *I wonder if that's the first time another child has been friendly to him*, Margaret thought.

After teaching the language class and the Bible class, Margaret again soaked Jiggerfoot's feet, speaking to him of

Jesus. Once more she worked painstakingly on pricking his toes to remove the terrible fleas.

Day after day Margaret worked and talked. Jiggerfoot stayed, saying little, but listening, she was sure. She told him about the true God and about His Son Jesus Christ. She talked about Jesus' many miracles and His terrible death and glorious resurrection. She talked about His power to save people from their sins.

"Would you like to learn some Bible verses that tell about some of the things I've been teaching you?" Margaret asked one day as she bathed his feet.

Jiggerfoot gazed at her in silence.

"Well." Margaret took a deep breath. "I'll teach them to you anyway. The first one we'll learn is John 3:16." To her surprise and delight, as she said the verse, Jiggerfoot repeated it after her. It wasn't long before he could say the whole thing himself. As he did, his face broke into a wide smile, his first real smile since he had come. Margaret took him in her arms and hugged him. He didn't seem to mind.

As the missionary worked on the infected feet, she taught the little boy one Bible verse after another. He spoke them and learned them quickly. He seemed to understand. He seemed to believe. And he held the stool and squeezed his eyes shut, saying the verses to keep from thinking about how much it hurt.

One evening Margaret said, "I'm all done now, Jiggerfoot. Look! The jiggers are gone! Your feet aren't swollen, and there's no more pus. You can walk. You'll have to get a new name, because you aren't Jiggerfoot anymore."

Jiggerfoot just looked at her.

"You can go home, but I know you don't have a home. Would you like to live here? You can come to my school and learn to read."

Jiggerfoot just looked at her.

"Well, I would be happy to have you stay as long as you like. I'll keep feeding you rice and bananas." She felt sure he would stay.

But the next morning Jiggerfoot said, "I am going now. Good-bye, Mama. Thank you."

He turned and ran off without another word. Margaret watched him go and suddenly felt hot tears running down her cheeks. *I felt so sure he would stay. Didn't he trust in You, Lord? Why would he leave like that? I love him!*

Three weeks passed, and Margaret's heart continued to ache.

Then one day, to her surprise, Margaret saw four new women sitting in the women's Bible class. She didn't recognize the tribal tattoo on their cheeks. "Where are you from?" she asked.

They named a village fifteen miles away. Fifteen miles? "Why did you come?"

"Are you Jiggerfoot's mama?" one woman asked.

Margaret's heart leaped. Jiggerfoot! Was he the reason they had come? "Do you know Jiggerfoot?"

All four women began to talk at once. "A dirty, rotten little thief!" one said.

"A scoundrel who broke our waterpots just to be mean!" cried another.

They went on and on, talking about what a nasty little boy Jiggerfoot was. Margaret's heart sank lower and lower as she listened. Hadn't he changed at all?

Then one woman said. "But that was all before. Then he was gone for a month, and we were glad. We saw him again, some weeks ago, and we all got our sticks to beat him and chase him away."

The others nodded vigorously. "Yes, but he began to cry out, 'Forgive me! Forgive me!'" said one woman. "We could hardly believe it!"

"And we said, 'Aren't you Jiggerfoot?' And he said, 'No! I used to be Jiggerfoot, but now I am Jesus' Boy.' And he told us about you, that you were his mama and you told him about Jesus and you showed him the love of Jesus.

"He said that you told him he could stay with you, and he was glad, but then when he prayed, God told him to come back to our village and ask forgiveness for everything he had done and become our servant." The woman snorted. "Think of us having a servant."

They went on to tell Margaret that Jesus' Boy had been true to his word. He had stayed in the village and while they were out working in the field, he had drawn their water for them and carried their wood for them. So they, in turn, fed him supper and sat with him around the campfire at night, listening to him recite the verses he had learned and tell them about the love of Jesus."

"And so we are here," they finished. "We want this God who changed Jesus' Boy's life to change ours too."

Over the next two months thirteen more women came. "Jesus' Boy told us about the love of God," they said. "We want our lives to be changed like his."

See Thinking Further for Chapter 6 on page 148.

7. CANNIBALS?

Mama Laird held tiny baby Marian in her arms and looked at her other two small children. "They want us to move to a land of *cannibals*?"

Life had changed for Margaret in the last five years. She had met Guy Laird, a missionary widower with a young son, and they had married and had two daughters of their own.

Now not just the children, but all the Africans who knew her called her Mama. She had been their reading teacher, teaching them bit by bit to read the Word of God in French.

But now , in 1928, the French government had new ideas for the missionaries.

"Mr. Eboue, the French administrator, says they're fine people," said Mr. Laird.

"Fine people? Cannibals?"

"But Mama," Mr. Laird said gently. "Don't they need the Lord too?"

Mama sighed. She knew he was right.

"And if the Lord wants us there, won't He protect us?"

"Oh, yes, I know He will, Guy. But I've never started out on something so dangerous with little children. And you know, I'm just not sure it's wise..."

"But where the Lord guides, He will provide, right?"

"Yes, I know that's true."

"We don't know what great things the Lord might have in store for us at Ippy. And the Bandas don't usually eat white people."

"Well, that's a great comfort, I'm sure."

"Mr. Eboue says they're just misunderstood."

"Misunderstood? I can't help but wonder if they're the ones who are misunderstanding something. When does he want you to go?"

"As soon as I can get ready. Thank God we have a truck now. I think it will take just a couple of weeks to scout out a place where we can set up a new mission station. Can you trust the Lord to watch over me while I'm gone?"

"Oh, yes, I can trust the Lord to do that. He even sees the sparrow fall." Mama's tone had a sharp edge to it that made her husband raise his eyebrows.

"Margaret." Mr. Laird held his wife gently. "Don't speak that way in front of the children. We are doing this for the sake of the gospel, for the sake of our glorious Lord Jesus Christ, to hear Him praised in the uttermost parts of the earth. And haven't we both been in danger before? He'll keep us as long as He has work for us to do. Pray for me."

Mama laid her head on Mr. Laird's shoulder. "I know. I know you're right. I'll pray. And yes, I'll try to pray in faith and not in fear."

Mr. Laird left and returned in a few days. "I had no trouble with the people," he said. "And I've found the perfect place for our mission station. Five springs on the land! We'll never lack water! Other people will come to us for water! Think of the opportunities!"

Kongi came to her side. "Mama," he said, "if you buy that herd of goats the other missionaries are selling, then you'll always have enough milk for your little ones, even in that strange land."

"Thank you, Kongi." Mama reached out her hand to the young man who had helped her so faithfully for five years. "But I have no idea how I would get those goats from here to there. They won't fit on the truck. And Ippy is three hundred miles from Bangassou."

"You can trust me, Mama. I will take the goats there for you. I'm a good goat boy."

Mr. Laird agreed and bought the goats. Before long he left again, to build the mud hut in preparation for his family. As Mama watched him go, she began to be filled with new doubts. *Are we being foolish, Lord? Are we just testing You?* She walked inside and looked at her three children, still sleeping so sweetly on their mats, Arlene's sweaty hair sticking to her face. *All these little babies. . . .*

Soon Kongi set out as well, driving a herd of valuable goats before him.

"Don't you think he'll take them away and sell them?" someone asked.

"No, I trust him." Mama Laird spoke with assurance. "He will keep them safe."

Then she heard her words coming back to her. *I trust him. He will keep them safe.* "Oh, Lord, I'm so sorry. I can trust my goat boy with a herd of goats. I know that I can trust You with my precious children."

Two weeks later Mr. Laird was back. By then Mama's attitude had completely changed. Through those two weeks she had wrestled against her own fearful heart and had come out on the other side, filled with faith and joy. "Did they receive the good news?" she asked eagerly.

"To tell you the truth, they mostly just ignored me," Mr. Laird replied. "I hired some men to help me build us a house, but most of the people paid no attention to me. The great chief of all those villages is dying, and they're all gathered at his village to wait for him to die. I suppose they're anticipating the great funeral celebration."

Mama Laird shuddered at the thought of what that funeral would be like.

"Mama," said Mr. Laird, "let's pray for that chief. If the Lord spares his life and we can help him, then that will open a door among the Banda people."

And so they prayed, asking the Lord to do great things, far beyond what they could imagine.

Then Mama said, "I have our things all ready, and the children are ready."

"Good. I think we can leave in the morning."

Mama hesitated. "Did you see Kongi on the way back?"

"No, I didn't see him. But you trust him, don't you?"

"Yes, I trust him."

Long before daylight the next morning, Mama climbed into the truck with Lawrence and Arlene and Marian. All their stuff was piled safely in the back. With the new roads and the new truck, the three-hundred-mile trip no longer lasted two weeks. "Praise God that we can do this in a day," Mama murmured. "Maybe we can make it before sunset."

Only fifteen hours later, the family finally climbed out of the truck. "Here's the place," Mr. Laird said. "Look around."

"I would if I could," Mama replied. "But between 'Here's the place' and 'Look around,' the sun set. It's pitch dark."

"It's hard to get used to an African sunset isn't it?" Mr. Laird chuckled. "Maybe you exaggerated just a little."

"It doesn't matter," Mama Laird said. "I trust you, and I'm sure it's good. But I'm exhausted, Guy. Can I go in the hut and rest?"

"Of course." He shone his flashlight on the small mud building. "But you see there are no doors or window coverings yet."

Mama led little Lawrence through the doorway and carried Arlene. Mr. Laird carried tiny Marian. They lit a lamp in the middle of the room.

But just as she began to relax, Mama realized that the house was surrounded with onlookers, standing at the doorway and on their tiptoes peering in at her. In the darkness she saw large white eyeballs and big white smiles. She gasped. "Guy! I thought you said the people ignored you!"

"Well, I said mostly," Mr. Laird replied. "To tell you the truth, the workers I hired did ask me some questions. They had seen white men before, you know, but they had never seen a white woman or a white child. They didn't believe there was such a thing. Turns out they thought white men were just the ghosts of their dead chiefs. So I promised when you came they could see you, to prove that we really are regular people like them."

"But do they have to see us now? I'm so tired!"

She turned to the window in exasperation. "Please go home!"

The people didn't move.

"I have to feed my children!" she said.

"Good," someone answered. "We will watch you."

"We need to go to sleep!"

"Good. We will watch that too."

Mama groped for an idea. "If you leave us alone, we will come out in the morning and wash the baby for everyone to see."

The little gathering murmured their agreement with this grand plan, and bit by bit they departed.

After a fitful night's sleep, Mama arose to find several Banda people already gathered to watch her wash the baby.

"I thought you said they were all watching the chief die," she muttered under her breath.

Mr. Laird just shrugged and smiled.

As Mama washed her baby, the Africans laughed with delight at seeing a real white baby, white all over!

So these are cannibals? Mama thought. *They seem like children.*

But then it was Mama's turn to laugh with delight. As she looked up the path, who should she see but Kongi, leading a herd of goats.

"Here, Mama!" Kongi called. "I didn't lose a single goat!" He put a jug into Mama's hands. "I milked the goats just this morning. Here is some milk for your little girls."

I can trust him! He will keep them safe! Mama's heart rose in song. *I can trust You, Lord. You will keep us safe.*

See Thinking Further for Chapter 7 on page 149.

8. THE MAN WITH A HOLE IN HIS CHEST

Mama groaned. "Oh, no. Do I have to ride on that thing?" She had never liked the push-push, and now it seemed especially bad.

"It's the best way to travel," Mr. Laird tried to encourage her. "It will get you to the chief's village quickly. And it's too soon after Marian's birth for you to ride your bicycle."

But the Banda boys smiling behind the one-wheeled contraption looked so small, and Mama felt her almost-six-foot frame towering over them.

"Big mama!" one of the young men exclaimed.

"Big *big* mama!" the other one agreed.

"Oh dear." Mama sighed. She rolled her eyes back at her husband as she put a coin into one boy's hand and climbed onto the precarious seat.

Forty-five minutes of bumping along the path, as the young men grunted and groaned, finally took her to Chief Yetaman's house. The Lairds had heard that yes, the chief was still barely alive, and yes, he wanted to see a white woman before he died. What a curiosity it was to see a white woman! The Bandas were learning that white men were not just the spirits of their dead ancestors.

But the chief's large mud-brick house stood empty. Mama coughed and cleared her throat to let someone know she was there, but no one came. She clapped her hands again and again. Still no one came. Finally she walked through to the other side. There, in the clearing, stood many more houses. "What are these?" she asked one of her drivers.

"Oh, big Mama, they are houses for the chief's wives. Chief Yetaman has seventy-five wives."

"So is he in one of those houses? Are they caring for him in there?"

"Oh, no, big Mama. His spirit will live in the house where he dies. So he is in the House of Death."

"I see," Mama muttered. "Nobody wants the privilege of having the dead chief live with her. So where is the House of Death?"

"Back there, Mama." One boy pointed beyond all the houses of the village.

"Then that is where I need to go." She looked at the push-push distastefully. "I'll walk," she said. The young men sighed and smiled.

Past all the houses of the village Mama walked, until finally she saw a small, forlorn hut. Dozens of people sat or stood in little clusters here and there around it, all silent as gravestones. They gazed at her with large, fearful eyes, but said nothing.

Floating out from the hut, Mama could hear a low, mournful chanting. *This is definitely the place,* she thought. *God, give me wisdom.*

Pushing the door open, she went in to find a pitiful looking old man, thin and bony, lying on a bamboo mat. Pus oozed from a large hole in his chest. Two women stood at his head, two at his feet, wiping the pus away with leaves.

The chief opened his eyes. "White woman," he moaned. "Why did you come to the House of Death?"

"I came to help you," Mama said. "I want to find out what's wrong. Maybe I have some medicine that will help you get well."

"No. No medicine will help me. Four French doctors have said I will die. Flee the House of Death. Save your medicine."

"But chief," Mama persisted. "How did you get that hole in your chest?"

"At the hunt," the chief replied.

Mama studied the hole. Then she understood. A wayward spear had struck the chief by accident. That meant this was just an infection. She had medicine for infections! The missionary felt a sense of great hope rise in her heart. "I think I can help you," she said. "I will come back."

Mama returned to the push-push as quickly as she could. "We must go back and come here again!" she told the drivers.

"Yes, big Mama." For forty-five minutes the drivers pushed her along the path, huffing and puffing. Then they waited as she ran into her home and quickly told her husband the news. She gathered her equipment, sterilized it, and returned to the push-push. For forty-five minutes the young men pushed her back.

Carefully Mama placed a rubber tube into the hole in the chief's chest. Then she ran two gallons of the antiseptic solution into his wound and back out again. Then she stood over him and prayed. "Oh Lord God! If it is Your will, raise up Chief Yetaman to health, so that the Word of God may prosper!"

The chief lay without a word. The women watched with fearful eyes.

"I'll be back in the morning, and tomorrow night," Mama promised.

It became part of the daily routine. Every morning Mama cleaned her equipment, prepared a new solution, and got ready to go. Every morning Mr. Laird summoned the push-push. Every morning Mama gritted her teeth as the drivers pushed her forty-five minutes along the path to treat the chief, and forty-five minutes back. In the evening, before the sun set, it was the same thing.

But one day the push-push drivers were nowhere to be found.

"Please let me ride my bike," Mama begged her husband. "I really think I can do it."

"Well, if you think so," Mr. Laird replied. "But don't push yourself too hard."

"Oh, I won't," she answered. "That's what those little boys have been doing all this time."

In less than an hour she was back. "It took only fifteen minutes on my bike!" she sang triumphantly. "I get hot, but it's worth it."

Every day the chief grew a little stronger. Every day Mr. and Mrs. Laird prayed together that he would be willing to hear the gospel. Every day, for two months, Mama biked back and forth.

Then one day at their doorway, there was the chief! He bowed down and held out a huge stack of French money.

"I want to pay the great white Mama," he said.

"Oh no," Mama gasped. "No, I didn't help you for pay. I helped you so that you can live to hear the good news we've brought. It was so we can show you the love of God."

"But I am a great chief! You must accept my gifts. Look!" Chief Yetaman pointed down the path. Now Mr. Laird gasped, and little Lawrence clapped his hands. There came a veritable parade of men bringing food: eggs, bananas, chickens, goats, pigs, and sheep.

"You must accept my gifts," the chief repeated. "This is the way we will know you are our friends."

Mama was speechless. But Mr. Laird answered wisely. "We don't want your money, but we will take your gifts. And we thank you with our hearts."

The chief seemed pleased. Mama was thrilled. Eggs! Meat! So many animals! Oh my, Kongi would have plenty to do now!

But Mr. Laird continued. "The best way you can show your gratefulness is to call all your under-chiefs to listen to my words."

Chief Yetaman turned and clapped his hands and spoke quickly to his people. They scurried away. Before long, the Lairds could hear a rapid beating of drums, sending a message over the entire area.

"How many chiefs are under Chief Yetaman?" asked Mama.

"I think it's about thirty," answered her husband. "And if they all come, you can be sure many of their people will come with them. He took his wife in his arms. "My dear! We are beginning to reap the great harvest of your hard work!"

"Let's pray!" Mama said urgently. "The enemy will rage like a roaring lion."

Together they fell on their knees, with Lawrence quietly between them, calling out to God to do a great work among the Banda people, for the glory of Jesus Christ.

It wasn't long before Chief Yetaman had gathered a huge crowd of people into the Lairds' clearing. "Who here thought you would see me again?" he cried out.

All the people bowed low, but they were packed so closely together that they bumped into each other. "We thought you were a dead man!" they all shouted.

"That I was," the chief replied in a strong voice. "But then this great white mama came with strong medicine. She came to the House of Death morning and night for many days with her medicine. She healed me."

I wish you'd say that God healed you, thought Mama. *But I guess that will come in time.*

"And now," Chief Yetaman continued, "This great white mama and her husband say all they want is for you to listen to their words."

Mr. Laird stood up and faced the hundreds of men who sat in a circle all around him. "I have come with great news from the true God," he proclaimed. "The true God is the God who made everything, all that you see around you." Silence greeted this statement, as the men looked around. The Lairds both knew this was a new thought to these men. But as she stood in the doorway listening, Mama prayed that they would think on her husband's words.

"The badness of men's hearts separated them from God," Mr. Laird went on. A low groan came from somewhere in the crowd. Mama turned her head quickly. Which of these men had been troubled by sin?

"But the true God had a Son who was God," Mr. Laird continued. "Because of His great love for us, He came to earth to die for our punishment. Then He conquered death. He can give new life to all who believe in Him."

This was enough for the first time. It would plant the seed. Mr. Laird sat down, praying that the soil would be plowed and the seed would take root.

Chief Yetaman stood again. "This white mama and her husband have come with good words," he stated. "So I command"—here he clapped his hands with authority—"that whenever this man or this woman come to your village, you beat the talking drums. Call everyone to come and hear what they have to say!"

See Thinking Further for Chapter 8 on page 149.

9. A VISIT FROM THE ELEGANT LADY

Mama's fingers flew to her flushed cheeks to hide the rising color. "Madame Eboue? Coming here to our house? For six weeks? With all three children?"

Mr. Eboue chuckled. "It won't be so bad, really, Madame Laird. She will greatly benefit from watching you and how you train your fine, strong children. And she gets so lonely and frightened when I have to be gone on these long business trips."

The French administrator had made the journey all the way to Ippy to talk with the Lairds and see the work they had accomplished. During the four years both families had lived in Bangassou, he had grown to trust Mama, having watched her as she cared for his sick children and even his wife in her illness. "You are not like many Americans," he said. "You know that I was the son of slaves, and yet you still treat me as your equal. My wife will be encouraged by your company."

"But . . . but . . . Madame Eboue is an elegant lady! I am a simple missionary living in a mud hut. Sir, the termites here are so friendly that they don't just live next door. They live right here in the house with us. What will Madame think when she sees that?"

"You act as if my wife has never seen termites. They are everywhere here."

"She may have seen them," Mama countered, "but has she ever seen them eating the mosquito netting right off from over her face? Has she ever watched them eat up a floor mat out from under her feet?"

"Madame Laird, you are exaggerating."

"Well, but not by much. And Mr. Eboue, in case you don't remember, I went to a great state dinner at your house. You served an eight-course meal on china plates with crystal

goblets! Look." She held up her dishes for him to see. "We serve simple meals on clay plates with clay cups."

Mr. Eboue waved his hand in disregard for her objection. "Nevertheless, Madame. Remember, I told you that you would be good for the people of Ippy? And look what you have done for them so far!" He spread his hands expansively. "You have worked your magic among them."

"Really, Mr. Eboue, you know how I feel about that kind of talk." Mama forgot her concerns about her house. "You know it is the Lord who has done this work."

"Yes, yes, to be sure." Mr. Eboue waved his hand again, as if he were shooing away a fly. "And so the Lord will do the work when you graciously welcome my wife into your home." He laughed.

Mama felt the color rising to her cheeks again. She nodded and bowed and said no more.

But when Mr. Eboue had left, she spoke again. "Oh, Guy!" she moaned. "How can I do it? A day maybe, but six weeks? What will I give her to eat?"

"She can eat whatever we eat," Mr. Laird comforted. "It will be all right."

"Where will they sleep? That's four more people in a two-room hut! We already have five of us living here!"

"I'll build her a bamboo hut out behind our house. They can sleep there. And we can make a schedule for the washroom. And Mama"—he turned her to face him—"don't worry about the food. The Lord is in this. You can be a shining light to Madame Eboue."

And so as Mr. Laird built the bamboo hut, Mama Laird prayed. "It's all just fear of man, isn't it, Lord?" she muttered. *The fear of man brings a snare.* "Oh, how I hate that! Don't let my feet be caught in that snare! Deliver me from fear of man!

"Proverbs 29," Mama muttered to herself. "What is the second half of that verse?" Then she found it. *The fear of man brings a snare, but whoso putteth his trust in the Lord shall be safe.* "Well, I could trust You with cannibals, Lord. Surely I can trust You with Madame Eboue."

It wasn't many days before the elegant black lady arrived with her two sons and little daughter. All of them were dressed in immaculate dress clothes, freshly starched and pressed. Madame Eboue, with her thick black hair perfectly coiffed, wore a white dress and white shoes. She even had on earrings. Mama inwardly groaned.

But the Eboue family, quietly and without complaint, moved into the bamboo hut behind the Lairds' house. Madame Eboue nodded as Mama explained the schedule for everyone taking turns in the washroom.

The very next morning, though, Mama forgot all her plans for the special supper she was hoping to fix. "Mama! Mama!" came the call. "Help!"

Mama raced out to the porch to see several Africans carrying two men into the yard. "Buffalo!" they called. Right away she knew what had happened. This was the season of buffalo hunts. These men had been attacked by a furious wounded buffalo.

Before she could do anything, one of the men died right before her eyes. The other had been slashed up his leg and tossed on the buffalo's horns. "Quick! Bring him in here!" she cried. She hastily swiped everything off the kitchen table and laid him there and began to clean the wound. All the way up his leg. She gritted her teeth as she began to dig out the gravel.

Madame Eboue and her three children stood in the back of the room with Lawrence, solemnly watching.

"Please," said Mama. "Prepare this antiseptic solution. Here are the directions." Madame Eboue obediently began to pour the boiled water into a pot and mix and stir.

Mama cleaned and swabbed antiseptic and stitched and bandaged. After several hours she finally said to the men, "Here, lay him on a mat on the porch. I want to be able to watch him." As four men carried their brother outside, she finally sat down to rest for a moment.

"We will eat simply tonight," she said.

Madame Eboue murmured an agreement.

The next morning, just as Mama was finishing baking the cornbread in her little stone oven, three women came running into the courtyard, yelling. "Mama! Mama! Help! Buffalo!"

"Oh, dear," Mama murmured. "Here, Madame Eboue, you get it out like this so you won't burn your fingers."

The elegant lady nodded, and Mama ran outside, only glancing at the man who still lay on the porch recovering from yesterday's adventure.

This time it was a little girl. "She burned her feet," the mother gasped, "so I set her in a tree until I came back from helping with the buffalo hunt. But then she thought the noise was me, so she jumped down, but it was a buffalo, and look what he has done!"

He had gouged her face, tossed her in the air, and gouged the other side. Once more Mama ran into the house, swiped everything off the kitchen table, and lay the moaning little victim on it.

"More antiseptic!" she called. Madame Eboue ran to obey.

Mama cleaned and stitched and bandaged, while Madame Eboue watched, just as she had the day before. But this time instead of a leg, it was a little girl's face, so Mama worked much more slowly and carefully.

After finally finishing the tedious work, Mama rubbed her tired eyes. Then she went outside to comfort the girl's distracted mother. "I think she'll be all right," she soothed. "Maybe her face won't even show the scars. But I need to watch her for a while. Let's keep her here for a day. She can lie on the porch." Mama looked back at the porch where Madame Eboue was taking a drink of water to the wounded man. "Good," Mama murmured. "Thank you, Lord."

Every day something happened. Every day there was a crisis. Mama barely even thought about the suppers.

Sometimes she was able to fix a little meat or eggs or bread. She hadn't yet had time to harvest and preserve anything from their garden here, but she thanked God for the canned goods she had brought from her garden in Bangassou.

Sometimes Mr. Laird heated up some canned cauliflower or beans over the stone fireplace after his hard day of work with the buildings. Sometimes even Madame Eboue prepared some food. But all of them were thankful simply to have something to eat.

"Mama! Mama!" Everyone was already in bed asleep when the cry came. "My sister!"

Mama ran out to the porch to see a woman alone, crying. "My sister delivered a baby that died, and now she is trying to kill herself!"

Without a word Mama ran after the woman through the darkness. She knew that to deliver a stillborn baby was such a disgrace that most African women would rather die than suffer the consequences of being cast out of the community. When she arrived at the hut to help the poor woman, she had heard a small noise. "It's the baby! It's not dead!"

Mama reached under her dress and tore off her slip. Then she gently took the tiny infant in her arms and carefully wrapped it. "Listen!" she soothed the sobbing mother. "I'll take your little one home and try to help it get better. You try to sleep."

Mama ran with the baby all the way back to her hut. "Guy!" she called. Mr. Laird was up, waiting for her return. "Quick! Do artificial respiration on this baby! I need to boil the needles!"

For hours the two of them worked on that baby, massaging it, breathing in its mouth, giving it shots. Finally when the baby was breathing well, Mama wrapped it again and placed it in a basket at the foot of her bed. Then she herself fell into bed exhausted.

Mama slept until well past sunup. "Oh, no! Breakfast!" she gasped, seeing the bright light out the window. While she hurried to prepare the food, Madame Eboue came in to wash for the morning.

But moments later she came running out again. "Madame Laird!" she called. "There is a wild animal in your bedroom!"

"What?" asked Mama, puzzled. "Did you see it?"

"No! I heard it! It is near the foot of your bed!"

"Oh, dear," Mama muttered. With Madame Eboue close behind, she ran into the bedroom. "Look, Madame," she said, pulling back the mosquito netting. "This is no wild animal."

Madame Eboue gasped. "How did that baby get there?"

"Madame, didn't you hear all the commotion last night?" Mama explained how the baby had come. The elegant black lady just looked at her and nodded, as if she were barely able to believe all the activity that went on in this little mud hut.

The day Madame Eboue was scheduled to leave, she stood before Mama with her three young children, all of them dressed in their best traveling clothes. "Madame Laird, you have been most kind," she began. "But I have to say that I think it is disgraceful what you are doing here. You lay injured people on your kitchen table, and sick people cover your front porch."

Mama felt her face burn with shame. "Madame," she finally said, "did you know that because I am an American the French government will not allow me to have a clinic here? That's why I have to do all the work in my home."

"That's ridiculous!" said Madame Eboue. "I will speak to my husband about this."

The administrator's wife was true to her word. Within days Mama received a telegram saying that she had been granted authorization to open an official clinic in Ippy—a separate dispensary where she could give out medicine. Within three months all the paperwork was in place for them to begin building it.

Mr. Laird looked over the forms with his wife. "And you didn't even have to fix one special meal to make it happen," he said.

"No," Mama replied. "The Lord made sure I didn't worry about that. He kept me so busy I never had a single moment to think about the fear of man."

See Thinking Further for Chapter 9 on page 149.

10. MANANGA THE WOOD AND WATER BOY

Mama waved her arm toward the east. "And yesterday, when I biked over to one of those villages over there," she said, "I was going over to care for that chief's wife, you know. But when I told him I had good news to tell everyone, well, the drum bangers grabbed their drums and started beating out the message telling everyone to come, and do you know that *three hundred* people came and listened to me? Kongi, we have an open door for the gospel!"

As she spoke, Kongi himself opened the door to the goat shed to let out all the goats for the morning, as he had been doing here in Ippy every morning for more than two years. He stood straight and tall, almost as tall as Mama now, watching them go bounding up over the hill. "It is good, Mama," he said. "They will soon believe in Jesus. I am learning too, from the teaching I get from your man every day."

"God is so good, Kongi." Mama shifted little Marian from one hip to the other. "We will see a harvest here. The fields are ripe."

"Mama!" came another voice. "Your water is all here." It was Mananga, the wood and water boy.

"Thank you!" Mama called. "Yes, you can go."

Mananga bounded away like the goats, heading for the chapel service that Mr. Laird taught every morning promptly at six o'clock. Kongi hurried to finish caring for the animals so he could run after him.

An hour later, right behind Kongi, Mananga was back. Mama had used some of the water for baths, so he quickly grabbed the buckets and ran almost half a mile back to the

stream to fill them again. Then he chopped wood for Mama to make the fire to boil the water she needed for drinking and cooking. In the afternoon, during the hottest part of the day, he rested while the family rested. But then he got back to work. On and on Mananga worked, chopping wood, carrying water, until five o'clock in the afternoon.

At five o'clock the drums beat the one-hour-till-dark warning. "Good-bye, Mama! I am going now!" Mananga called.

Mama sent Lawrence out to drop a coin in his hand. "Good-bye! Thank you!" she called back. She was busy with her children and her supper and barely noticed the wood and water boy as he ran off.

Life was getting established in a routine here in Ippy. The Lairds had become accepted as welcome members of the community. Mr. Laird had hired over a hundred men to help him make bricks and build a large brick chapel building so that by the time the rainy season came they would be able to sit in a strong, dry shelter. As they anticipated the coming of the rains, they prayed for spiritual rain in the hearts of the people, to help the Word of God take root and grow.

Now, after almost six months, the chapel would be finished in a few days.

So one Sunday, all five of the Lairds and Kongi joined the hundreds of Bandas who had come for the dedication. After the singing and the preaching and the prayer, Mr. Laird raised his voice. "Tomorrow," he said, "we will have a special meeting, a new kind of class. It will be only for any of you who have understood our words and trusted in the perfect righteousness of Jesus Christ for salvation. If you have really repented of your sins and believed in Jesus as your Savior, we want you to come to this class. We will teach you more about how to live the Christian life and walk the Jesus road."

A low murmur passed through the crowd as people whispered to each other. Mama wished she could hear them. Had they understood her husband's words? Would anyone return the next day?

The next morning the two missionaries and their children walked down the hill, both of them eager to know how many Africans thought they had really trusted in Jesus.

But when they arrived at the chapel, they stopped in confusion. It was full! There were just as many people there as had attended the dedication service the day before!

"They didn't understand," Mama murmured.

"No, I guess not," said Mr. Laird.

"Who are those people? They're not Bandas." Mama

nodded toward fourteen very tall men sitting in the front row. Each one was several inches taller than the tallest of the Banda people.

"I don't know," whispered Mr. Laird. "I've never seen them before. This is very strange."

He walked to the front, while Mama stood to the side with the children and watched. "My friends," he said, "This class is only for people who have put all their trust in the complete righteousness of Jesus Christ and want to know how to walk the Jesus road. Maybe some of you made a mistake. We will stand and sing a song, and if you haven't trusted in Jesus and want to walk in His way, you can leave."

What can wash away my sin, they sang. *Nothing but the blood of Jesus.* They sang with their eyes closed and their hands raised.

Then, after the song, they sat down again. All of them were still there.

Mr. Laird cleared his throat, trying to figure out what to do. He finally decided to sit down and talk with each person one by one to hear their testimonies. Mama joined him as he began with the tall men in the front row.

"Greetings, my friends," he said.

"Greetings," they replied. "We are from the Sara tribe."

"Welcome." Mr. Laird shifted uncomfortably. "What has brought you here today?"

"This class you have offered," said one. "We have trusted in Jesus Christ. We want to walk the Jesus road."

Another man closed his eyes and said, "You are saved by grace, through faith. It does not come from yourselves, but it is God's gift. It is not of your own works, or you would boast." Then he added, "That is from the book of Ephesians."

Mama was astonished. Where had they learned Bible verses? "Perhaps another mission work came to their village," she whispered.

Mr. Laird nodded. "What mission are you from?"

"Mission?" they asked. "Mission?"

"Well, uh, where is your village?"

"On the other side of the woods behind your house."

"That's at least three miles by the road," Mama said.

"How did you learn about Jesus?" Mr. Laird finally asked.

"Mananga has taught us!" All the men nodded vigorously.

Mananga? The wood and water boy?

"Yes, Mananga comes every night and teaches us about the love of Jesus."

Every night?

Mama hurried back up the hill to her house. There was Mananga. He had left the meeting and was chopping wood to light Mama's fire, singing a little song under his breath.

True riches of life, true riches of life,

In Jesus you will find true riches of life.

"Mananga!" Mama called. "Come here."

"Yes, Mama?" The teenage boy came quickly and stood smiling.

"Mananga." She looked at him as if she were seeing him for the first time.

"Yes, Mama?"

"Have you been going to the Saras' village?"

"Yes, Mama."

"When do you go?"

"Every night when the drums beat."

"But, but, you can't get there and back before dark!"

"Oh, I get there just as the sun is dropping," Mananga explained. "I tell them about the great love of Jesus, and they are eager to hear. Many, many are coming to listen to my good words. I teach for maybe two hours each night. Then we visit for a while, and I come home about midnight."

"You come home at midnight?" The story seemed stranger and stranger. "I wonder how you have so much strength to work during the day, but I wonder more about your safety. What about all the lions and leopards and hyenas and poisonous snakes that are out at night? You know that wild animals have killed people here, not even that long ago!"

Mananga gazed at Mama, and for a moment he didn't answer. When he did, he sounded as if he were talking respectfully to a small child.

"Mama, why did you come to our land?"

"Well, you know. To tell you the good news of salvation through Jesus Christ. To offer your people freedom from the slavery of sin."

"And Mama, did you know that we ... we were people-eaters?"

"Yes. Yes, of course we knew that."

"Did you know about the leopard men?"

Mama had seen one of those men. Now that cannibalism was against the law of the French government, some men dressed as leopards at night to steal goats and sheep, and yes, even babies.

"Yes, I knew."

"But were you afraid to come?"

"No." Mama answered truthfully. "By the time we got here, I was not afraid. I knew God would protect us. He has promised to keep us safe, as long as He has work for us to do." Suddenly her face flushed red as she realized what she was saying.

But Mananga spoke anyway. "Ah, Mama. You can trust the true God to keep you safe among the people-eating tribes. And just the same, I can trust the true God to keep me safe among the people-eating animals. Your God is my God now. And the good news of the love of Jesus Christ must go out to all the people, all around. Not just when it seems safe, but all the time. The good news must go out."

See Thinking Further for Chapter 10 on page 150.

11. MISSIONARIES FROM CANNIBAL COUNTRY

One morning Kongi stood before Mama with his hands on his hips. "Mama, you'll have to find a new goat boy," he said. "I'm not going to watch the goats anymore."

Mama stuttered, searching for words. As much as she had tried to prepare herself for this event, it still hurt. "You've served us faithfully for a long time, Kongi," she finally said. "I thought there might come a time when you'd get homesick. You can go back to Sibut."

"Homesick?" Kongi snorted. "What do you mean homesick? I'm not going back to Sibut! Weren't you listening to your man this morning?" Kongi pointed as if he could see through the thick undergrowth and tall trees all around them. "He talked about all the other tribes in this land who have never heard of Jesus. He said that the missionaries are starting a school to teach young men to be evangelists to the other tribes, and I want to go to that school. So I won't have time to watch the goats."

Kongi stood straight and tall. "I want to be a missionary like you."

Mama's eyes filled with tears as she gazed at this young man. But how could she be sad? Kongi was ready to go.

It was happening more and more as the months passed here at Ippy. Young men were leaving. Ever since the missionaries had finally translated the Gospel of John into Sango, many Banda people were taking it in as life-giving food. So many people of Ippy had become Christians in the past year. Mama's new believers' class was full of young men and old people and even children longing to learn to read so that they could read the Word of God.

Some people learned quickly. After the full-time classes Mr. Laird offered, many of them left for the Native Workers' Bible Training School at another mission site. Kongi left. Mananga, the wood and water boy, left.

But some were slower learners. Reading seemed like such a mystery to them. They knew that the marks on the paper said something, but they had a hard time figuring out just what it was. But even in these people, the fire of the gospel burned with a desire to take the good news to those who had never heard.

"Mama." It was Mako, one of Mr. Laird's most faithful students in the Word of God. "I am not doing right. I have fallen on my face before the true and living God. I have known Jesus Christ and His great salvation. But here I am, singing of Jesus, living in His love, while in my own village far away, there is no light. They are in darkness. I will take the light to them."

"Have you spoken to Mr. Laird about this, Mako?" Mama asked. "Does he think you're ready to go?"

Mako shrugged and held his arms wide. "Yes. God tells me to go. I hear His voice even when I sleep at night. How can I stay here?"

And so the next day the family watched as Mako headed out and disappeared down the long road and behind the trees. "Will he be all right?" Mama wondered. "He can barely even read."

"Maybe he didn't tell you this," Mr. Laird replied. "But in our classes he has memorized the entire gospel of John. He has a great message to tell, and a great burden to tell it. He'll be safe in the arms of our loving God."

Many months later the Lairds heard the rest of the story of Mako's mission work.

He had returned to his native village and gathered the people. "I have great news!" he cried. "You no longer have to be enslaved to the spirits! The great God has sent One to free you!"

Every day after their work, many people gathered in a clearing to listen to Mako preach. Though he knew very little of the Bible, he understood enough to tell them the good news of salvation. And he repeated the gospel of John over and over and over. The fire in his heart caught hold in the hearts of others. They began to memorize the gospel as well. One by one, the people of his village began to fall on their faces before the true and living God and confess their sins and claim Jesus Christ as their great Savior.

But time passed, and Mako knew he could not keep teaching his brothers and sisters. "Oh, God, I know so little!" he cried. "Please send us another teacher!" He promised his people that God would be faithful to send someone to disciple them.

More months passed. The people met together every day. They listened to the gospel of John. They sang the hymns Mako had taught them. And they prayed. More and more they spent time in prayer. "Oh God, send the one that we need! Send our brother with more light! Send us one to teach us!"

One afternoon after the singing and the reciting, Mako could bear the waiting no longer. He fell on his face and

began to sob. For some minutes he sobbed before he could even speak. The people gathered around him, moaning and groaning. "Oh God!" he cried. "I have trusted You! I have believed in You! But I have asked You for so long to send us someone to teach us more about Your true and living Way, and You have not! I have asked you to send someone to teach us to read, and You have not! I know You are faithful! What shall I do, O God? What shall I do?" His whole body shook with the sobs.

Suddenly Mako felt a hand on his shoulder. He turned and looked, and there stood a man holding a Bible. For a moment, Mako only stared. Then, without speaking a word to the white stranger, he turned back to lay his face on the ground once more. "Oh God!" he cried. "Forgive me! I doubted Your love! But all along You had someone prepared to come. Oh thank You, God! Oh thank You!"

The young man was Richard Paulson, another missionary with Baptist Mid-Missions, who had wanted to go someplace in Africa where the name of Jesus had never been heard. The Lord had led him to this village where he thought there was no gospel witness. When he came and heard singing that sounded like a hymn, he could hardly believe his ears. The singing, and then the praying, had led him to this clearing.

So much work had already been done. Seventy-five people had already put their faith in Jesus Christ. In a very short time Mr. Paulson helped Mako establish a large mission work in that area, with a church that sent out its own evangelists. God had shown Himself faithful once again.

See Thinking Further for Chapter 11 on page 150.

12. GOTTA WORK SUNDAYS

A chunk of chewing tobacco flew out of the foreman's mouth as he spat vigorously. "You fellas from Ippy?"

"Yes, sir." Eleven men stood before him.

"I know you're smarter than the average Africans, and you take orders better." The men stood silent. "And you're honest." The foreman's jaw moved up and down. "That's why I got you working in key places. That's why you're working in my kitchen and in my tool shed and in my office instead of working in the mines." He jabbed his finger at different men as he spoke. "You know that, don't you?"

The men nodded slightly. "Yes, sir."

"But now you got me all stirred up." The foreman began to pace back and forth like a rooster looking over his hens. "You won't work Sundays. I let it go for a while, because I liked your work. But I can't let it go no more. Everybody's gotta work Sundays. The boss is telling me he wants the gold faster, see?" He thrust his thumb over his shoulder. "So now you gotta work Sundays."

The eleven men stood silent for a moment. "Sir," one of them finally said, "we are the people of God. Sunday is the day of God. We must have that day to read our Bibles and pray. We will work for you diligently every other day, from the time of sunup to sundown. But we must have that day to rest and worship."

The foreman spat again on the ground. "Okay, here's what I'm gonna say. If anybody in this camp won't work Sundays, he can just go to the office at the end of today and pick up his last paycheck. He won't be working for me no more. You got it?"

"Yes, sir." The men looked at each other sadly.

"I hope you fellas will see some sense."

"Yes, sir." They turned and walked away.

At the end of the day, when the foreman was shuffling papers in his office, first one and then another of the eleven Ippy men walked in. "I am here for my last paycheck, sir," each one said.

"Hey, you fellas!" he cried. "I thought you were gonna see some sense!"

"Yes, sir," they said. "Thank you, sir." Each one loaded his pack on his head and started walking the long road back to Ippy.

The foreman went to the door and watched them go. "You can just get outta here then, and good riddance!" he shouted. "And take that Christianity with you!" He turned and glared at all the other workers, who were watching with open mouths. "What's the matter with you!" he shouted. "Get back to work!"

The next day an important man came to visit. The foreman called one of his house servants. "Get us a big spread for lunch," he said.

"Sir," came the answer, "your cook is gone. You sent him away."

The foreman muttered under his breath and barked orders to fix something anyway. The lunch was a long time coming, the meat was burned, the gravy was lumpy, and the bread was soggy.

Then the foreman took his guest out to the gold mine to show him some of the work. But not a single miner was working. Everyone was sleeping.

"What are you doing out here?" The foreman shouted.

"We have no tools," one man complained. "How can we work? All we could do is sleep."

"What do you mean, you have no tools?" The foreman's face turned bright red with anger. "Why do you have no tools?"

"We stopped by the tool house to get the tools this morning," one man explained. "But you sent away the man in charge of your tool house, remember?"

"I remember," the foreman hissed between clenched teeth.

"And he gave the keys to another man, and that man got drunk last night and left the toolhouse unlocked, and somebody stole all your tools. So today we cannot work." The worker shrugged.

Another man said, "The only ones who took care of your things were those Christians from Ippy. The ones you sent away."

The foreman made a motion in the direction of that worker, almost as if he would strike him. But he strode away without even offering an apology to his guest.

All the way back to the camp he marched. Then without a word he climbed into his truck and drove as fast as he could on the road toward Ippy.

There they were. "Hey, you fellas!" he called. They turned to look. "Get in the truck, you're coming back to work for me."

"No, sir," they said.

"You don't have to work Sundays. Just get in and come back." He turned off the engine and worked his jaw up and down as the men looked at each other.

Finally one man spoke. "Sir, we have been walking for many hours now. And we have had much time to think and talk and pray. This is what we have decided. You know that every Sunday we meet, just us, while all the other men are working. But we want to work at a place where all the men have Sundays off, so that we can have someone to preach to. And we want to have a chapel to meet in like Mr. Laird has at Ippy. So wherever we go to work now, those are the things we want."

The foreman stood in the truck, both hands on his hips, chewing and spitting for all he was worth. His face blotched with anger, and he spat out his words. "All *right*. Just get in the truck and come back." He turned and sat down and started the ignition.

But the Africans didn't move yet. "There's one more thing, sir. At Ippy we had the Lord's supper once a month. We want to ask you to get the white missionary from Moroubas to come. We know it is far, but we think he would come if he had enough gasoline. So if you'll take him some gasoline for the trip every month, we'll come back."

The foreman's shoulders slumped. "They know when they've got me," he muttered under his breath. "All right," he said. "Get in."

A few days later Mr. Vanderground, the missionary at Moroubas, looked up with surprise to see a man unloading two huge drums of gasoline from his truck. "I didn't order that," he said.

"No, but I guess your God did," came back the sarcastic reply. "And if you'll come to hold a meeting at my gold mining camp once a month, I'll deliver you two barrels of gas every month to do it. Seems like your God and me, we got a fight going on. And so far, it looks like He's winning."

See Thinking Further for Chapter 12 on page 151.

13. KONGI THE MISSIONARY

It just wasn't the same Kongi. This bitter, angry young man couldn't be the same person as the happy little goat boy who had given his life to Jesus, or the stalwart young disciple who went off to Bible school, determined to become a missionary.

But that was before the leprosy. Now in his late twenties, Kongi had lost five toes and could barely walk. The leprosy was beginning to spread over his whole body. Mama had biked to his village back and forth, back and forth, twenty miles each way, to give him injections twice a week, but they hadn't helped. She had even brought him back to Ippy to care for him, but he was no better.

"Kongi," Mama finally ventured one day, "the only leprosy colony in this whole area is back in Sibut, near your old home."

"Are you telling me to leave?" Kongi sat in a ball, his knees hunched up to his chin.

"It isn't that I want you to leave me," Mama continued, almost helplessly. "It's just that I can't really give you what you need. The leprosy colony will have more medicine for you, and better medicine, and doctors who have been trained in just the right way to treat leprosy, and. . . ."

"Oh, yes," Kongi answered bitterly. "The missionary mama loves her little goat boy when he is well and strong, but when he—"

"Kongi!" Mama raised her voice. "Don't talk like that!" *Don't you see what I've done for you because I love you now?* she almost said. But she bit her tongue and turned her words to Jesus.

"Don't you see," she said tenderly, "that God has called you to Himself, and given you the opportunity to be trained in His Word? Don't you see that He has put His love in your heart? Don't you see that He may still have a mighty work for you, even in the leprosy colony?"

Grudgingly, Kongi packed his bag and climbed on the back of the next mail truck, headed for the leprosy colony at Sibut. As Mama stood and waved, he didn't even look up.

"Oh God!" Mama prayed. "I pray not so much for the healing of his body as for the healing of his heart!

"And please," she added, "please give me an opportunity to go visit him there."

Every day Mama prayed for her little goat boy, but many months passed before she was able to make the almost two-hundred-mile trip to visit the leprosy colony at Sibut.

Though Mama had seen many terrible sights in her days working as a nurse among the Africans, the deformities she saw all around her here made her feel overwhelmed. She tried not to stare at one misshapen body after another. "Oh, Lord Jesus," she cried in her heart, "we can't work miracles of healing the way You could when You walked the earth. But You are still the miracle-working God. Bring hope to these people who must feel as if they are past all hope."

"What can I do for you?" A nurse in a white uniform greeted Mama.

"Uh, I'm looking for Kongi, a young man who came here from Ippy."

"Oh, yes, Kongi," answered the nurse. "We all know him. That is his hut." The nurse pointed to a small building that people appeared to be streaming to from all directions. "We call it the social hub of the colony." She chuckled and went on her way.

Mama could hardly believe her eyes—or her ears, either—as she approached. Loud laughter issued from the hut. More than one person laughing. And one of them, oh, she thought one of them sounded like Kongi. She hadn't heard his laugh in so long.

"Mama!" he greeted her with a face wreathed in smiles. "It is so good to see you! It is almost time for the afternoon meeting. Come meet my friends!"

Mama was introduced to first one and than another of Kongi's friends, in various stages of the disease. Every pair of eyes, no matter how misshapen the face, showed forth joy. "Kongi, is this what you have done?" Mama asked in a whisper.

"Oh, Mama, you know you don't say that!" Kongi laughed. "This is what *God* has done. You remember you told me that He may have a mighty work for me in the leprosy colony?"

Mama nodded wordlessly.

"I remember you, Mama." The voice came from below, near Mama's feet. The missionary looked down to see a woman crawling toward her, so eaten up with leprosy that she barely looked like a person.

"Oh, Mama," the woman cried. "Don't look at me like that!" She turned her face upward more, and Mama saw that her eyes had the same glow she had seen in the others. "I thank God I have leprosy!"

What?

"I will tell you my story," the woman said. "Years ago, when you lived in Sibut, you came to my village on your bicycle and told us about God and sin and Jesus. But I spat on your shadow. I was such a beautiful girl that I thought I didn't need your Jesus. I scorned your God. Other missionaries came, and I spat on their shadows too.

"I married the chief, so I became even more proud. But then the leprosy covered my hands and feet, and I was turned out of my village. No one wanted me. Not my husband. Not my parents. No one.

"The leprosy ate away my hands and my feet, and covered my beautiful face so that it became the ugliest face in the world. Then I came to this colony. I wanted to die."

The woman had been smiling as she spoke these terrible words. But now her smile grew even bigger. "Then Kongi came. I complained to him, I told him my bitterness, but he said he understood, because he had felt it too. Then he told me about the One who cares even when no one else seems to care. Mama, this time my heart was open to Jesus Christ. This time I knew I needed the love of God. I could trust in myself no longer." Her eyes filled with tears. "And he told me about you, Mama, the big white woman on the bicycle. Without a doubt I remembered you."

As Mama knelt down and drew close, the woman continued. "If God had never done this, I never would have learned about the love of Jesus. I know I will have a new body in heaven, but if I had kept my beautiful body on earth, I would never have listened to the gospel. So I thank God I have leprosy."

"Mama!" Kongi called. "Will you speak at our meeting?"

With tears in her eyes, Mama spoke about the amazing love of God, the great hope of salvation, the overflowing joy of Jesus, and the assurance of eternal life with Him. The lepers, none of them healed but all of them thankful, gazed at her with light in their deformed faces, murmuring agreement with every word.

When Mama finally left the hut, an African man in a white starched uniform came to greet her.

"Are you Madame Laird?" he asked. "I have wanted so much to meet you!"

Mama nodded. How did he know? What other wonders could God have in store on this amazing day?

"I am a doctor here. And Madame, I want you to know that I received the very best training in Paris, and I was a brilliant student. So you can suppose how angry I was at being stationed at a *leprosy* colony! I thought of these people as nothing better than animals." He chuckled.

He turned and walked with Mama as he continued talking. "One evening I saw that many people were gathering in that hut right there." He pointed to Kongi's hut. "I thought, oh no, they are up to no good. So I looked in the window and I saw one of them take out a little black book and start to read it. I thought 'one of those tribal animals can *read*?' But it was your Kongi. He was reading the Bible to those people. And then I listened to him talk, and Madame, I was astonished at the depth of his learning. I was raised in a church, but I had never heard that Jesus died for my sins. I began to realize that *I* was the animal!" Here he turned to look at her, pointing to himself. His great laugh came from deep down, but tears stood in his eyes. "I was the one who needed something, and Kongi was the one who could give it to me. Kongi showed me Jesus Christ, and I was gloriously saved. Almost everyone here counts it a privilege to live at this leprosy colony."

"And look." He reached into his pocket and pulled out a small black book. "Look at what he gave me. It is very, very special."

Mama reached out to take the little New Testament. She opened it to the front and read, "To my dear boy Kongi, from Mama. 1924. Keep loving Jesus."

* * *

God did heal Kongi of his leprosy. Though his scars remained, the leprosy left his body. He continued serving and preaching in that leprosy colony for twenty more years.

See Thinking Further for Chapter 13 on page 151.

14. MANANGA THE MISSIONARY

The villagers stood with open mouths, listening to Mananga preach. "Cast away your fetishes!" he shouted. "They have no power to help you! They will only bring you into greater bondage!"

"What about the crucifix?" one person asked. "It has power, doesn't it?"

"No!" Mananga's voice thundered. "The only way you will find true peace and freedom is through Jesus Christ!"

The people of the villages were afraid. The priest had forbidden them to listen to the words of the missionary Mananga. But Mananga's words were so different, so amazing, so powerful that more and more people kept coming to hear.

All through his four years of training at the Native Workers' Bible Training School, Mananga had yearned to take the gospel to people who had never heard. God had given him a promise from Psalm One. "You will be like a tree." Deep roots. Much fruit. Prospering. These are the promises that sustained Mananga as he trusted God alone to provide for him and his family through the years he studied.

Now in some villages, hundreds of people were gathering in the clearings to listen to this young man preach the story of salvation in Jesus Christ, great and free.

That evening, though, two drunk men came to listen. As soon as Mananga finished preaching and the crowd had left, these two men approached him. "Preacher!" they called. "Christian preacher!"

When Mananga turned to face them, the two men grabbed him and began to beat him with their clubs. They beat him until they thought he was dead, or nearly so. Then they dragged him to the edge of the clearing and left him for the leopards to find after dark.

This was where three men found Mananga hours later. But he wasn't dead.

"Could you take me back to Bambari, to my home?" he gasped.

Without delay, the men carried Mananga the four miles to Bambari, where several years earlier Mananga and his wife had helped Mr. Laird open a new mission station.

Mananga had been trusting God to make him strong like a great tree, but now he was in bed at the Bambari hospital, gasping with pain.

"Your spine is broken," the doctor proclaimed. "You will never walk again." Mananga's wife and children gathered around him, and began to quietly cry.

Before long, the administrator of the hospital came to Mananga's room. "We have found the two men who beat you," he said. "What would you like me to do with them?"

Mananga gazed up at the administrator. He thought for a moment.

"Would you please bring them here so I can tell them about Jesus Christ?"

The administrator raised his eyebrows. "These men tried to kill you," he said. "And they almost did. They left you for dead, and maybe it would be better if you had indeed died, because the doctor says you will never walk again."

"But they didn't know what they were doing. The liquor made them go out of their minds. Now if they are sober, I want to talk to them."

The administrator didn't try to hide his surprise, but he brought the men to Mananga's bed.

"You are great sinners," Mananga spoke through his pain. "But I have good news for you. I was a great sinner too, and

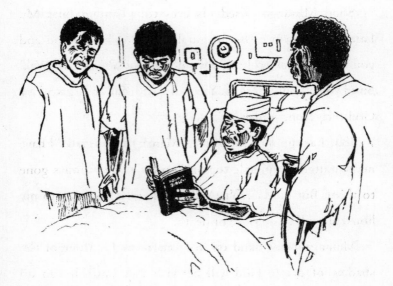

Jesus Christ saved me. I am free from my sin through His blood. That cross that the priest tells you to pray to—that is nothing. But the true cross of Jesus Christ offers great hope. He died to save sinners. He rose to give new life to sinners. Believe on Him, my friends."

Mananga read the Word of God to those two men, who stood with their heads down the entire time. When it was time for them to go, they left, without a word, to return to the prison. The French administrator led them out. He had been listening.

Just a few days later, a telegram was sent to the Lairds. "Mananga has tuberculosis in his spine," it reported. "He will not live long."

Soon Mananga raised his eyes to see Mama and Mr. Laird standing over his hospital bed. "We'll take you and your family back to Ippy, Mananga," said Mr. Laird. "We'll build you a house near us. You can still speak of the work of God even from your bed."

"But I am going back to die," Mananga answered. "I have never waited for people to come to me. I have always gone to them. But now I can't. And people won't come into my house. It will be a house of death."

Mama put her hand on his. "Even in the valley of the shadow of death, God will be with you, and He can do great things," she said. "Cry out to God. Until you die, ask God to bring you people to hear His Word. He will be faithful."

* * *

Several years passed. The Lairds had an opportunity to visit in the home of a high French official. It turned out to be the very same man who had been the administrator in the hospital where Mananga had stayed.

"How long did that man live?" The administrator asked. "What happened to him?"

"Oh, what a good story that is!" Mama said. "I will tell it.

"We built a house for Mananga across the road from ours, and of course it was a 'house of death,' because the doctor had said he was going to die, you know, so naturally the natives would avoid his house. But Mananga began praying that God would bring him people to speak to about the Lord Jesus Christ, and wouldn't you know it, a stream of people began flowing in and out of that house! I was teaching a class for new believers, and every time people came that I didn't know, I asked them where they had come from and how they came to the Lord, and I think nearly three hundred people came into that class who said they had come to salvation on their knees at the bed of the man who lived in the house of death!

"And I wish Mananga were here tonight to tell you this story himself, but we left to go back to America for several months, feeling sad that he could never walk again, of course, but lo and behold when we got back, what do you think? There he was walking around as good as new! He said—" and here she deepened her voice—" 'Mama, the day came when no more people came into my house. I cried out to God that if I couldn't speak about Him I wanted to die. Then I thought, God, You are the God of the universe, and You can raise me up to go out where the people are. And I called to Him, and He answered, and I've been walking ever since.' Ha! He recently even asked to borrow my bicycle and told me that when God heals a man's back it's strong enough to go biking as well as walking!" Mama clapped her hands for sheer joy.

"Sir," Mr. Laird said quietly, "I want to talk to you about your own soul. Have you ever trusted in this Savior that Mananga knew and that we know?" He pulled out his New Testament.

"No, but I want to," the man replied. "Read to me."

Mr. Laird read many Scriptures, while the French official nodded with tears in his eyes. Before long he got down on his knees with Mr. Laird to ask God to forgive his sins and save him through the power of the blood of Jesus Christ. When they rose, all three of them were shedding tears of joy.

"Now I have my own story to tell you," the official said. "Please listen.

"Ever since I met that man in the hospital bed, I have stood in awe. From the time he asked to speak about Jesus Christ to the men who tried to kill him....I can't even describe my feelings. I had never seen love like that. I left the hospital that day determined to do some research. As you know, I am a man of research. The very first research I did was to walk to the mission station and buy a New Testament. Here it is." He reached into a little drawer beside the chair where he sat and pulled it out. "I read this New Testament from cover to cover, and I have been reading it every day since. The Scriptures you read to me tonight were very familiar to me.

"Then I did some more research by walking the road Mananga had walked the day he was beaten. I spoke to the people all around. All of them knew who that missionary man was. And because of his beating—because of his beating, I tell you—more and more of them were turning to Christ, and more and more were becoming bold for Him, even in the face of persecution. I spoke with many different tribes, and some of them I knew had harbored hatred for each other for years. But all of them loved Mananga, and they were coming together in a way that seemed to me to be miraculous. The only word I knew to describe it was love. Then I knew there was power in the gospel of Jesus Christ.

"Mr. Laird. Madame Laird." He looked at them both earnestly and tapped himself on the chest. "You have never in your life seen a man who was more ready to give up his self-righteousness and turn to Jesus Christ than this man has been tonight. The life of Mananga turned my heart."

See Thinking Further for Chapter 14 on page 151.

15. YOU NEED A HOSPITAL

The voice kept screaming in her head. "He's dead! He's dead! Those French doctors don't care. Don't care! *Don't care!*" Mama buried her head in her hands.

"And God doesn't care!" the voice continued. "Look at all the good your man did! Look at how he gave his life for God. And now he's gone! Just like that! Couldn't God have saved him?"

"Oh God," Mama sobbed. "I'm in the middle of a battle right now. It seems like a battle for my very soul. Please, oh God, keep me from becoming bitter against You."

Part of what that voice said was true. Some of those French doctors didn't care. They had told her that her husband was in perfect health when really he was dying of sleeping sickness. By the time he finally got to a doctor who actually knew what he was doing, it was too late. Guy Laird was buried in Ippy, in the spring of 1946.

Part of what that voice said was false. She knew it. God really did care. She knew it. God cared. God cared. *As for God, His way is perfect.*

Mama headed back to the United States, on the trip she would have taken with her husband. Sitting on the airplane, she thought back over the twenty-one years of mission work

they had together. It seemed too short, far too short, even though much had been accomplished. She closed her eyes and pictured her husband hunched over his little printing press, his shirt sleeves rolled up, working late into the night printing off pages of the gospel of John in Sango or pages of the Sango hymnbook. She remembered the great joy in his face as he showed her the very first bound copy of the Sango New Testament. "Mama, the Word will go forth with power!" he had said. She thought about how he had comforted her in her discouragement trying to teach the new believers to read.

Lord, You are my Comforter. You will sustain me through this darkness.

But one thought kept coming back to her mind. *You need a hospital at Ippy.* "Oh, God, maybe I'm thinking those thoughts just because I feel angry that Guy didn't get the help he needed. Please forgive me." But the thought kept coming back. *You must have a hospital at Ippy.* "What a blessing that would be," Mama said to herself. "I've had this dispensary for all these years, but no doctors." She sighed dreamily. "How wonderful that would be." *You must have a hospital at Ippy.* "Yes, Lord," Mama finally prayed. "When I get back to the U.S., I'll ask them for it."

But the leaders of the mission had not had the same thoughts she had been thinking. "A mission start a modern hospital? Mrs. Laird, as much as we respect you, we have to say that you aren't thinking rationally about this. The cost would be enormous. And remember, we are a *faith* mission."

Mama remembered. Hadn't she been living by faith all these years? Hadn't she and her husband always trusted the Lord to meet their needs? But hadn't they seen the Lord provide for them again and again, in miraculous ways? What about *that*?

The men went on. "And then, we would have to trust the Lord not only for the building itself, but for the doctors. Think of it. Would there be people who give the best years of their lives to train to be doctors who would then be willing to join a faith mission?"

And why wouldn't there be? Mama thought. Guy was a highly qualified engineer who gave the best years of his life to God. He gave all of his life!

"And then," the men went on, "what about all the equipment a modern hospital would need? Thousands of dollars' worth of equipment. There is no way that a faith mission can take on such a thing."

What a big fool you turned out to be! The voice came back. Mama left that meeting feeling as if she must have completely misunderstood the will of God.

Back in her room, Mama paced up and down. "Oh God!" she cried. "I need some reassurance from You! Please lead me from Your Word! I need something to stand on, Lord!"

Second Kings chapter seven. The story of the four lepers outside the city? The men were only lepers. And she was only one woman.

But God is powerful. *When it looks as if everything is dismal and there is no hope, God can suddenly turn everything around.*

Mama went to the meeting the next day filled with new hope.

"Will you allow me to speak in churches about this need if they invite me?" she asked.

"Well, yes."

"And if people send money marked for the Ippy Hospital, will you put it in a special fund for that?"

"Well, certainly."

"Then that is all I ask." Mama felt her burden lift, and her face broke into smiles. "We'll see what God will do."

A missionary friend invited Mama to come to a church in Kansas City. When she arrived and met the pastor over Sunday dinner, he asked her to tell him about her ministry.

Mama began to talk about life among the cannibals in the heart of Africa. She told him about Kongi and about Chief Yetaman and about the work her husband had done.

The pastor was fascinated. "Tell me more," he said.

So Mama told him about Mananga and Sultan Hetman and the Ippy missionaries.

The pastor could barely eat his dinner. "Tell me more," he said.

So Mama told him about doing medical work in her mud hut and Madame Eboue and getting a dispensary and the need for a hospital.

"Mrs. Laird," said the pastor. "I have never heard anything like this. Please come speak to our young people in their class this afternoon."

Mama did. Afterward, the young people surrounded her with questions, so that by the time she got to the evening church service, she had to sit in the very back of that very large building.

When the service was almost over, before the closing prayer, the pastor stood silent for some moments. "Brothers and sisters," he said. "There is something on my heart, and I can't close this meeting. We have a woman of God in our midst tonight." Mama's face was flushing red. Was he really talking about her? Then he said, "Deacons, will you give me permission to allow this woman to speak?" He paused. "Mrs. Laird, will you rise right where you are and take five minutes to speak what is on your heart?"

What in the world? Five minutes to speak what's on my heart? Here in a seat under the balcony? God help me!

Mama rose. She spoke. Afterwards she couldn't even remember what she had said. But she knew she said something about the hospital.

The next morning, before Mama left, the pastor called her into his office. "Mrs. Laird, we have never heard things like this before. We'd like to give the first five thousand dollars toward your hospital."

Months passed, and Mama spoke in one church after another, telling of the great things the Lord had done, speaking about her vision of the great things He had yet to do. Bit by bit the money for the hospital came in. Over obstacles that seemed impossible at first, that hospital began to rise. In less than five years it was completed. And yes, God provided the money for the equipment, and even doctors who had given the best years of their lives to study medicine.

Besides being able to help the local people better, the new medical facility provided something surprising. A whole new mission field opened. European men, coming to Africa to hunt "big game"—elephants, lions, and tigers—sometimes ended up on those hospital beds. These were people Mama would never have even seen if the hospital hadn't been there.

When one Frenchman, supposedly the greatest elephant hunter in Africa, went to the Ippy hospital, his life was so radically changed that he took the good news back with him to the place where he was working in Africa. Almost every week Mama saw someone at her door, asking how to be saved, saying he had been sent there by the elephant hunter.

One day Mama heard a cough at her door. "Mama!" the voice called. "It is Panyaka!"

Mama opened the door to see a man she remembered well. She had treated Panyaka in her dispensary years ago, and he had faithfully sent money to her mission ever since he left Ippy.

"I have come to open a store near your hospital, as I promised," Panyaka said.

"Come in, come in!" Mama cried. "It's so good to see you, Panyaka! But opening a store here will bring you far less money than staying near Fort Crampel. Are you sure you want to do this?"

"You know I do." Panyaka's face split into a smile. "This is where I want my sons trained, and I can preach the gospel to the patients' relatives when they come to your hospital. Oh, Mama, it is so good to see you again! Do you remember when I first came to you?"

"Oh, do I!" Mama laughed. "How could I forget! You were the orneriest young man I ever tended in my dispensary!"

"I remember!" Panyaka laughed with her. "I said to you, 'Wash me if you must, but keep your big mouth shut!' Oh, Mama, can you ever forgive me?"

"You can't know how many times I wanted to open my big mouth and snap your head right off," Mama replied. "So I guess you'll have to forgive me too. At least God did help me to keep my big mouth shut."

"Oh, no," said Panyaka. "You opened your mouth in words of love and hope. That is how my work among the Mandji tribe got started. It is because of the words of life you brought to me. That is why the work there now has so many believers. Praise God for your big mouth."

See Thinking Further for Chapter 15 on page 152.

16. THE SULTAN'S PRAYER

Sultan Hetman, dressed immaculately as always, sat in the large armchair across from Mama. "The doctors said I am dying, Madame Laird." He looked thin, she thought, but otherwise she wouldn't have known he was sick. His short black hair was flecked with a distinguished gray. The year was 1964.

"You've done so much good in this great country of yours," Mama said. "Your position of power has gone a long way to spread the gospel. Your money…"

Sultan Hetman waved his hand. "What I have done is insignificant. It is what *God* has done that we will proclaim." He pulled out a piece of paper from a drawer. "I want to tell you, Madame Laird, how I have planned my funeral."

Mama closed her eyes, imagining the funeral that this man's father must have had, the three hundred women who had followed him into the grave.

"My mother, Madame Laird, was a piece of property, bought and sold like an ox. She had no choice but to follow her husband into the grave. Indeed, my mother knew only a life of despair."

My mother knew only a life of despair. Mama's thoughts flashed briefly back to her own mother, who had prayed for a missionary child. Through the years as Mama had sent letters, her own mother's life, back in Colorado, had been turned from sadness to a joy that overflowed, telling others around her of the great work that God was doing in the heart of Africa.

"My wife," the sultan was saying, "will not perform these pagan practices at my death of shaving her head and stripping off her clothes and turning somersaults and shrieking and wailing. I want no eulogy. My funeral will be a time of rejoicing and proclaiming the gospel of Jesus Christ. I want all the people of my country to know that they can trust in His righteousness and His alone. Look, I have chosen these hymns to be sung, and I have asked the preacher to deliver the most powerful gospel message he has ever spoken. I have asked him to be filled with the power of the Holy Spirit. I have told him to offer an invitation to come to Christ.

"I want to be like Samson." Sultan Hetman chuckled at Mama's quizzical look. "But different in one important way. I pray to God that through my death more people will come to Him than they ever did through my life."

* * *

A few weeks later Sultan Hetman was buried. His one and only wife, breaking from the traditions of African widows, wore her most beautiful dress and welcomed people with a gracious smile, without shedding a tear.

Over three thousand people gathered for the funeral, including high officials of the country, even the president of the new Central African Republic. The sermon that was preached proclaimed the gospel with such power that even before the invitation was given, people left their seats to come to the front. Many people in the audience stood, asking

to be allowed to give testimony of how Sultan Hetman had led them to Christ.

The people didn't talk about how the Sultan had given so much money to the churches. They didn't talk about how he had used his power to open the doors to Christianity. They talked about how he had shown them the love of Jesus.

Mama sat back in her chair and closed her eyes while she listened. It all sounded similar to other words she had heard. She herself had been honored before crowds, even while she still lived. But was it for teaching French and Sango? Was it for raising money for the district? Was it for opening the first hospital in Ippy? No. Instead, these were the words she remembered:

"She always had extra babies in her house, raising them and feeding them. . . ."

"When we came running to her, she always helped us. . . ."

"She brought me into her house with her son and gave me cocoa. . . ."
Mama thought back to the story she had heard in church many years ago of a shy little button girl who spoke in love to a prominent, intimidating businessman and wouldn't give up. What was important? It was the love. The shining forth of the love of Jesus Christ.

The good news must go out.

See Thinking Further for Chapter 16 on page 152.

THINKING FURTHER

Chapter 1 — A Mother's Prayer

Joel 2:25-26 I will restore to you the years that the swarming locust has eaten, the hopper, the destroyer, and the cutter, my great army, which I sent among you. You shall eat in plenty and be satisfied, and praise the name of the LORD your God, who has dealt wondrously with you. And my people shall never again be put to shame.

What does it mean to ask the Lord to "restore the years the swarming locust has eaten"?

How does God sometimes use the mistakes we have made to accomplish His purposes?

Chapter 2 — The Button Girl and the Street Sweeper

Luke 12:16-21 And he told them a parable, saying, "The land of a rich man produced plentifully, and he thought to himself, 'What shall I do, for I have nowhere to store my crops?' And he said, 'I will do this: I will tear down my barns and build larger ones, and there I will store all my grain and my goods. And I will say to my soul, 'Soul, you have ample goods laid up for many years; relax, eat, drink, be merry.' But God said to him, 'Fool! This night your soul is required of you, and the things you have prepared, whose will they be?' So is the one who lays up treasure for himself and is not rich toward God."

Sometimes God's people are afraid to wholeheartedly follow Him because He might ask them to do something that they don't want to do. If you understand that He is our loving Father who knows and wants the best for us, how will this change your attitude about following Him?

Mr. Flacks went from being very successful and wealthy to being very poor, doing the lowliest of jobs. Yet he was very happy. What does this teach us about the things that make us truly happy?

How was Mr. Flacks similar to the fool in Luke 12? How was he different?

Chapter 3 – Third Class

1 Corinthians 13:4-5: Love is patient and kind; love does not envy or boast; it is not arrogant or rude. It does not insist on its own way; it is not irritable or resentful.

What was the lesson of love that Mr. Haas taught Margaret?

Why was Sango the language the missionaries needed to learn in order to reach the people?

Chapter 4 – Kongi the Goat Boy

Philippians 4:11b I have learned in whatever situation I am to be content.

I Corinthians 9:19, 23 For though I am free from all, I have made myself a servant to all, that I might win more of them. I do it all for the sake of the gospel, that I may share with them in its blessings.

If Margaret had said, "I'm God's child and I won't live in a goat house," what opportunity would she have missed?

What is a trial in your life or your family's life that God has used for new opportunities?

Margaret apologized for complaining. In what way was she really not a complainer?

What did Kongi do or say to show that Jesus had changed him on the inside?

Chapter 5 – The Two Sultans

2 Corinthians 5:17 Therefore, if anyone is in Christ, he is a new creation. The old has passed away; behold, the new has come.

When she left Sibut to go to Bangassou, Margaret was stepping out on a new adventure of faith. What words of encouragement would you have given her as she set out?

What kind of surprise did Margaret receive when she met Sultan Hetman? Why do you think he was so different from what she expected?

How did the life of Mr. Haas affect the entire country?

Chapter 6 – Jiggerfoot

John 13:3-5 Jesus, knowing that the Father had given all things into his hands, and that he had come from God and was going back to God, rose from supper. He laid aside his outer garments, and taking a towel, tied it around his waist. Then he poured water into a basin and began to wash the disciples' feet...

Who washed feet in the Bible? How was Margaret's work similar to that story?

How did Margaret know what to say to Jiggerfoot as she worked on his feet?

Why do you think so many women came to Christ because of Jiggerfoot?

Chapter 7 – Cannibals?

Psalm 4:8 In peace I will both lie down and sleep; for you alone, O LORD, make me dwell in safety.

Why was Mama afraid?

Do you think this was a reasonable fear? Do you think you would have been afraid in this situation?

How did Kongi remind Mama of God?

Chapter 8 – The Man with a Hole in his Chest

2 Corinthians 12:15a I will most gladly spend and be spent for your souls.

How was Mama's life "spent" for Chief Yetaman? What was her goal in working so hard?

How were the talking drums used by God? What are some other instruments or tools that can be use by God to spread the gospel?

Chapter 9 – A Visit from the Elegant Lady

Proverbs 29:25 The fear of man lays a snare, but whoever trusts in the LORD is safe.

Mama had been around cannibals and was no longer afraid of them. Why was she so afraid about Madame Eboue?

Sometimes God uses difficult circumstances to prepare us for a special blessing. How did God do that in this chapter?

Chapter 10 – Mananga the Wood and Water Boy

John 4:35b-36 [Jesus said] Look, I tell you, lift up your eyes, and see that the fields are white for harvest. Already the one who reaps is receiving wages and gathering fruit for eternal life, so that sower and reaper may rejoice together.

There were several surprises in this chapter. What were some of them?

What were some excuses Mananga could have used if he had wanted to rest at night?

What did Mananga need to have in order to be an effective missionary?

Chapter 11 – Missionaries from Cannibal Country

1 Cor 9:16 For if I preach the gospel, that gives me no ground for boasting. For necessity is laid upon me. Woe to me if I do not preach the gospel!

Mako had memorized the whole gospel of John. Why was it important to also have someone who could read to help teach them?

Mako and his people had to wait a long time for the answer to their prayer. Why do you think God sometimes lets people wait so long?

Chapter 12 — Gotta Work Sundays

Matthew 11:28 Come to me, all who labor and are heavy laden, and I will give you rest.

Jesus Christ had given the Christian men rest from their sin. How did they want to celebrate that rest?

How did God bless the eleven men's determination to do right? How did He give them even more?

Describe what your thoughts and feelings would have been if you had been the missionary, Mr. Vanderground.

Chapter 13 — Kongi the Missionary

Romans 8:28 And we know that for those who love God all things work together for good, for those who are called according to his purpose.

Getting leprosy is a terrible tragedy. How was Kongi's experience an example of Romans 8:28 at work?

Why did the young woman think leprosy was a blessing in her life? Can you think of someone in the Bible or in history who went through tragedy to find great blessings?

Chapter 14 — Mananga the Missionary

Matthew 5:44-45 But I say to you, Love your enemies and pray for those who persecute you, so that you may be sons of your Father who is in heaven.

How did Mananga show Christ's love to the ones who had tried to kill him?

God doesn't promise that the people we show love to will come to Christ. But in Mananga's situation, someone else did. How did that happen?

Why was the hospital administrator impressed with Mananga? How was he impressed with the people Mananga had preached to in the villages?

African beliefs meant that people would be afraid to approach a house of death. How was Mananga's situation a miracle?

Chapter 15 — You Need a Hospital

Psalm 18:30 This God—his way is perfect; the word of the LORD proves true; he is a shield for all those who take refuge in him.

Sometimes God takes us through a very dark time to accomplish something great. What was Mama's dark thing? What did God want to do?

An *ironic* situation is one that is the opposite of what it seems like it ought to be. How was the reaction of the faith mission leaders to Mama's request ironic? What did Mama have about this situation that they didn't have?

Chapter 16 — The Sultan's Prayer

Philippians 1:20-21 As it is my eager expectation and hope that I will not be at all ashamed, but that with full courage now as always Christ will be honored in my body, whether by life or by death. For to me to live is Christ, and to die is gain.

How did Sultan Hetman and his wife break from their culture in order to show their hope and joy in God?

How did God use Sultan Hetman's life and death to bring people into His kingdom?

What was more important to people than the great accomplishments of God's workers?

ABOUT THE AUTHOR

One of Rebecca Davis's favorite things to do is to discover little-known missionaries who have amazing stories about the wonderful works of God. Sometimes the missionary stories are self-published, sometimes published by a mission board, or sometimes in a notebook stuck away in a drawer. She loves to take these stories and write them in a way that children and their parents can enjoy them together.

As a member of the South Carolina Storytelling Network, Rebecca also loves to tell stories from her books, for children's churches, home schoolers, Christian schools, and family gatherings. Through her dramatizations, she seeks to help the children and their parents catch a fresh vision for the mighty power of God in the lives of His people, and the great salvation available through Jesus Christ.

ABOUT THE MISSIONARY

In 1922, Margaret Nicholl became one of the first missionaries to travel to the heart of Africa with Baptist Mid-Missions, newly formed by William Haas specifically to take the gospel to central Africa. With her nurse's training, her French language study (because the area at that time was a French colony), and her Bible, Margaret and a few other missionaries rode a steamship up the Congo River to the area that became known as the Central African Republic. Later marrying Guy Laird, Margaret continued the work until her retirement in the 1960s, becoming not only one of the first, but also one of the longest serving missionaries with Baptist Mid-Missions.

While they were in the French colony, the French government decided to take advantage of the missionaries' boldness, asking the Lairds to go to live among a tribe of cannibals in order to gain their trust. The French cared about the gold mines they had discovered in the area. But the Lairds cared about the souls of men, and so they settled in the village of Ippy, where the Lord worked a mighty work in changing hearts.

The stories in the children's book *The Good News Must Go Out* are based on Margaret Laird's own personal reminiscences in *They Called Me Mama*. Like its predecessor, *With Two Hands,* it focuses not only on the western missionary, "the great white mama," but even more on the national missionaries, the people of Africa who come to Christ and feel the burning longing in their hearts to take the gospel to those around them who have never heard.

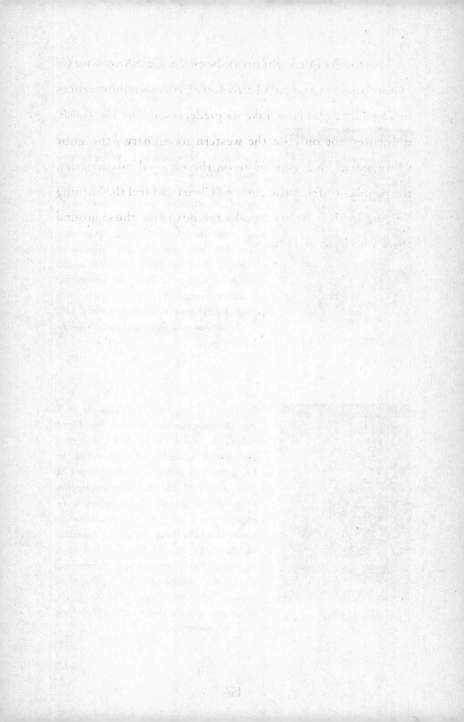

MORE HIDDEN HEROES
by Rebecca Davis

ISBN: 978-1-84550-539-4

Why would a crippled old man wait by the side of the road every day for twenty years? Why would a slave and a witch doctor walk for three days to find a man called Jesus? Why would a lame man purposely walk to a tribe where he knew he could be killed? Sixteen captivating episodes from one Christian mission in Ethiopia show the power of God in the midst of darkness. Find out about the invisible evangelist, the two girls who prayed and other astonishing stories. This is a book that will make you gasp at God's goodness!

ISBN: 978-1-78191-515-8

In 1938, in the remote highlands of a mountainous island, explorers discovered thousands upon thousands of tribal people. Missionaries began to come, to bring the Good News of the Gospel of Jesus Christ. Little did they know that many of the people of the tribes were waiting ... waiting ... for someone to come and help them out of the darkness of their old way of life. Witness Men consists of true missionary stories that took place throughout the highlands of Papua, Indonesia, from 1955 to 2010, when one of the tribes received their first New Testaments.

ISBN: 978-1-78191-292-8

The hill tribes of Southeast Asia told legends that one day the White Book that their ancestors had lost would be brought back to them. When the Karen tribe saw the Bible in 1813 through the mission of Adoniram Judson, they recognised the White Book of their stories. This is the amazing true story of how the faith spread through the land of Myanmar, formerly Burma.

ISBN: 978-1-78191-409-0

Colombia has been known as a land of violence – Colombian people have reacted to the Gospel of Jesus Christ by cursing the messengers, beating them, kidnapping them, killing them and burning down their houses. But God has delivered people from burning houses. God has healed the ones who cursed. God has even rescued kidnappers. Read fourteen true stories of the Light of the World shining in the land of Colombia, South America.

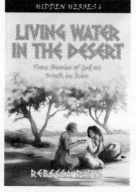

ISBN: 978-1-78191-563-9

More Muslims in Iran have come to faith in Christ in the last thirty years than in the thirteen hundred years that Islam has been in the country. In a land that is notorious for persecution, through the lives of missionaries and Iranian believers God's Word is being spread far and wide. Seventeen chapters tell true stories of the Living Water of Jesus Christ pouring out for thirsty people to drink in the country of Iran.

CHRISTIAN FOCUS PUBLICATIONS

Christian Focus | Christian Heritage | CF4K | Mentor

Christian Focus Publications publishes books for adults and children under its four main imprints: Christian Focus, CF4K, Mentor and Christian Heritage. Our books reflect our conviction that God's Word is reliable and Jesus is the way to know him, and live for ever with him.

Our children's publication list includes a Sunday School curriculum that covers pre-school to early teens, and puzzle and activity books. We also publish personal and family devotional titles, biographies and inspirational stories that children will love.

If you are looking for quality Bible teaching for children then we have an excellent range of Bible stories and age-specific theological books.

From pre-school board books to teenage apologetics, we have it covered!

**Find us at our web page:
www.christianfocus.com**

CF4 •K
*Because you're never
too young to know Jesus*